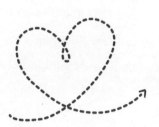

ALSO BY REGINA BRETT

God Never Blinks

Be the Miracle

God is Always Hiring

REGINA BRETT

LITTLE DETOURS

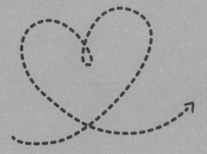

and SPIRITUAL ADVENTURES

*Inspiration for Times When Life
Doesn't Go As Planned*

GRAY & COMPANY, PUBLISHERS
CLEVELAND

Gray & Company, Publishers
www.grayco.com

ISBN 978-1-59851-136-9
1

Contents

Contents

Contents

To Asher, Ainsley, and River
My sacred three
My perfect joy

Introduction

Just when you think you have it all figured out, life pulls a switcheroo on you.

The road zigs when you zagged. Your hopes and dreams come to a dead end or a screeching halt or you just simply run out of gas and feel stranded on the highway of life or you end up feeling lost and alone because you ran out of map for whatever happens next.

It could be a divorce, a diagnosis, or a death. Or the hole that was your childhood of abuse and neglect keeps opening to swallow you and all the joy around you.

You feel empty and alone. Confused and forgotten. Abandoned and forsaken.

You are not alone. C. S. Lewis wrote that people read to know they are not alone. I wrote this book to remind you that you are not alone in your loneliness. Someone else has been there. Someone else has shared that same hole in their heart, the one that feels so deep and endless it creates a hunger nothing seems to fill, a hunger so familiar to us all.

Years ago in Ireland, I stumbled upon a postcard with words from Irish poet Patrick Kavanagh: "We are not alone in our loneliness / Others have been here and known / Griefs we thought our special own . . ."

I carried it around for years like a note from a lover. Someone knew my pain. Someone knew my soul. Someone's words matched the hole in my heart and made me feel whole. What a relief.

For much of my early life, I felt even God wasn't aware of my existence. It was as if the moment I was born, God blinked and missed the occasion. Many years of therapy, recovery meetings, and spiritual retreats taught me God never blinks.

That became the title of my first book, which hit the *New York Times* bestseller list and was translated into 24 languages. The first lesson in that list of 50? *Life isn't fair, but it's still good.*

It still is, despite losing countless friends and family members, in spite of wars and poverty, in spite of global warming and a global pandemic.

I still believe that life is good, even when it isn't fair.

I still believe every detour that life gives us becomes a spiritual adventure to strengthen our soul to better love ourselves, our lives, and everyone in it.

I still believe God never blinks.

That's why I wrote this book, to help you believe, in spite of it all. To help you take the spiritual aerial view and see all those detours as spiritual adventures. To remind you that you are never lost, and you are never alone.

I share my experience, strength, hope, and humor as I navigate the detours of life. I also share stories of others who faced bigger detours than I have and still created a life they love out of it all. People who found the awe in the awful, the mystery in the mistakes, the magic in the mess.

The Universe led you to this moment, this detour, this book. I hope it comforts you, challenges you, and empowers you to choose love as a response to every life detour.

I hope on every page you feel celebrated, understood, heard and seen, and more loved than ever before, because you are.

1

Life handed you a winning lottery ticket. Play it.

Gambling isn't my thing, but I have won the lottery more times than I can count.

Maybe you dream of winning the lottery. The truth is, Life already gave you a winning lottery ticket. You're sitting on it. No, it's not under your chair. I'm not Oprah so you don't get a free car or a trip to Disney.

You get something better.

The lottery tickets I'm talking about don't look like winners.

Your lottery ticket could be buried under your deepest shame. Mine was.

My family was BIG on religion. I come from a devout Irish Catholic family. We had a three-foot-high crucifix over the TV set in the living room, a huge, framed print of the Last Supper in the dining room, rosaries tucked under the bed pillows, and an almost life-sized statue of the Blessed Virgin Mary in my parents' bedroom. It looked like a church blew up in our house.

So when this "good" Catholic girl ended up pregnant at 21, it was a real shocker. I was a student at Kent State University, and I was on the parish council at Immaculate Conception Church (insert cringe).

How to tell my parents? I was a coward, so I wrote a note and stuck it under a refrigerator magnet. (Insert longer cringe.) I dropped out of college. My parents let me stay at home to get on my feet and loved being grandparents. That baby girl I had was the greatest gift of my life. Still is.

When my daughter turned 6, I went back to college so I could better support her as a single mom. After changing my major six times, I finished a 4-year degree in 12 years, graduated Kent State at age 30 and began my career as a journalist. In time, I wrote about being an unwed mother to make it easier for the next woman and her family.

Decades later, a woman who had heard my story introduced me to a friend, Sharon, who was in her 20s, was single and pregnant, and needed support.

I'm like, that's MY ticket! I got the unwed mother ticket!

I met Sharon and invited her over for dinner to meet my daughter. They became great friends. That Thanksgiving, I invited Sharon to join us. Thanksgiving morning, she called and asked, Can I bring my brother? Of course. Hours later, in walked Sharon and her brother, James, a handsome man with piercing blue eyes.

My daughter married him three years later.

My three grandchildren have those eyes. Their aunt is Sharon, the woman who got my lottery ticket. Her son is their cousin.

It's amazing what happens when you play your lottery ticket.

Your lottery ticket could be tucked inside your greatest challenge. Mine was.

I didn't marry until I turned 40. A year later, I found a lump in my breast. Stage II breast cancer. The fast-growing kind. The oncologist explained my three options: surgery, chemotherapy, and radiation. Which do I get? All of the above, he said.

My chemo cocktail consisted of Adriamycin, Cytoxan, and a drug called 5-FU. I think every cancer-fighting drug should be called F-U. I was going to lose my hair 14 days after that first chemo.

I bought a human hair wig and took it to a salon to style it to look like my hair so the world would never see me bald. The salon ruined the wig and wouldn't return my calls.

Meanwhile, my hair was falling out. I was eating cereal, and suddenly my Cheerios had bangs. When I finally got the wig back, I couldn't wear it. They had over-permed it and ruined it. It looked like roadkill.

So I went boldly bald. But most days I didn't feel so bold. When I went to see the musical *Beauty and the Beast,* a child in front of me kept turning around to stare at me. I wanted to say, "The Beast is up there!"

After I survived cancer, I tried to turn my powerlessness into power for others. I started giving speeches to cancer survivors. I spoke at a fundraiser for the Cancer Services of Northeast Indiana and saw they had a free wig salon!! I took photos, showed them to the head of The Gathering Place, a support center in my hometown, Cleveland, and urged her to create one. I gave her the money from my speeches for seed money.

We grew three free wig salons, one on the East Side, the West Side, and at MetroHealth Medical Center in Cleveland. You're going bald from chemo? That's my lottery ticket! I can't cure cancer, but I can make the journey a bit easier.

Your lottery ticket could be hidden under an avalanche of grief. Mine was.

I have five brothers and five sisters. That's ten lottery tickets! People always ask, where are you in the line up? I'm five of eleven—which sounds like the *Star Trek* character, Seven of Nine. Yes, we had our own football, baseball, and soccer teams.

My parents did their best, but there was never quite enough Mom to go around. Imagine doing laundry for 13 people every week. Our basement dirty-clothes piles looked like the Appalachians of laundry.

My deepest wound was that I never quite felt a mother's love, never felt that mom/daughter connection. Most of my life I felt hungry for it. Starving.

So when my mom got Alzheimer's at the end of her life, I figured that bond was never going to happen. Turns out, it was another sneaky lottery ticket.

She asked me to take her to doctor appointments. We had endless trips to Dairy Queen after each one. In time, I found a memory care unit for her.

While caring for her, I met and came to love the woman I never knew inside the mom who was so busy raising all those kids. I also came to love the girl inside that woman, a girl who had once felt as bruised as I did.

My mom played her final lottery tickets at that nursing home: She crocheted hats for the homeless. Slippers to warm the feet of children she never met. Prayer blankets for chemo patients.

My mom never stopped serving, never stopped scratching off her lottery tickets, never stopped making everyone around her feel like a winner.

So what's your lottery ticket?

Your lottery ticket could be a difficulty, a diagnosis, a disappointment. It could be a failure, a flaw, or a part of your very identity that you struggle to accept.

You know what it is.

It's up to you to decide that your darkest secret or greatest challenge or deepest wound is no longer going to be your liability. It is your lottery ticket.

Your lottery ticket might be Parkinson's or your mom's Alzheimer's or your son's autism. Your lottery ticket might be bipolar disorder or depression or alcoholism.

The truth is most real lottery tickets are losers. You scratch them off, feel unlucky, and toss them out. But with a life lottery ticket, when you use it for others, no one loses.

Whatever you have been handed in life or will be handed in life, there will always be something you don't want. Something you wouldn't choose. Something the Universe needs you to share so you can be of service and heal some corner of the world.

My friends in recovery taught me this beautiful promise that turns their sordid past into someone else's sacred gift: "We will not regret the past nor wish to shut the door on it."

We're all sitting on a life lottery ticket. You can choose to make it the greatest gift that you give the world.

How?

Name it. Identify it. Deep down inside, you know what it is.

Claim it. Accept it. Befriend it. Embrace it.

Play it. Share it. Blog about it. Write about it. Create art around it. Volunteer around it. Let it inform and inspire your work.

Because you didn't come to planet Earth to make A difference.

You came here to make *your* difference.

Life handed you a lottery ticket. Play it and you make you—and everyone around you—a winner.

2

It's time to glow up.
The world needs your light.

Sometimes the world feels so full of darkness and despair, it can be overwhelming.

The war in Israel. The war in Ukraine. The poverty. The political division. The fake news. The deaths of dear family and friends. You almost hate to open the newspaper, turn on the TV news, or sign on to Facebook.

There's an old saying that it's better to light one candle than to curse the darkness. That's really all it takes is one candle, one light, to dispel the darkness.

What if *you* were the light?

Author Elizabeth Gilbert, who wrote *Eat, Pray, Love,* challenged me with that question after I read her article about being stuck on a crosstown bus in New York City during rush hour. It was originally published in *O, the Oprah Magazine,* but I found it on Facebook.

She writes about an unpleasant bus trip through clogged traffic in Manhattan where everyone on the bus was cold, tired, and grumpy. As the bus approached Seventh Avenue, the bus driver got on the intercom and announced to everyone on board:

"Folks, I know you've had a rough day and you're frustrated. I can't do anything about the weather or traffic, but here's what I *can* do. As each one of you gets off the bus, I will reach out my hand to you. As you walk by, drop your troubles into the palm of my hand, okay? Don't take your problems home to your families tonight—just leave 'em with me. My route goes right by the Hudson River, and when I drive by there later, I'll open the window and throw your troubles in the water. Sound good?"

Everyone burst out laughing. Was this guy for real?

Yep. At the next stop he opened his hand and waited.

Some of the passengers laughed and a few cried, but everyone dropped an invisible something into the palm of his hand. The bus driver did it at every stop, all the way to the river.

She wrote that the world is a difficult place to be in, that we all have bad days that can last a lot longer than a day—maybe for years. At some point in life, we all struggle and fail when it comes to work, finances, friends, faith, and, of course, at relationships.

"There are times when everything seems cloaked in darkness. You long for the light but don't know where to find it," she wrote.

Right there, pause. You can relate, right? We all can.

And here's the part that felt like some Great Force lit a pilot light inside me:

"But what if *you* are the light? What if you're the very agent of illumination that a dark situation begs for?" she wrote.

One year I visited lighthouses all along Lake Erie. We in Cleveland call it the North Coast. A sign at Marblehead Lighthouse honored the lighthouse keepers and called them *The Keepers of the Light*. I love those words.

That's what we all are. Keepers of the Light. But so much gets in the way of us shining our light to help others. All our personal wants and desires for the future shut us off from enjoying what is right in front of us. All our fear of failing keeps us from shining what light we do have.

To glow up, you have to release those blocks that cut off the light. As I visited each lighthouse, I released one thing that blocked the light in me. I found a rock, paused, named what I wanted to release, and gave that rock a fling into the Great Lake in front of me. Splash!

I let go of productivity, of being too busy to be present. Here's to choosing presence over productivity. Splash!

At another lighthouse, I tossed in FOMO: Fear of Missing Out. No more feeling that where I'm at or what I'm doing and who I am isn't enough. Splash!

I released what other people think I should be doing with my life and my time. Splash!

I un-shamed my life and set free all those "shoulds." No more "should-ing" all over myself. Shame *off* me! Splash!

At the last lighthouse, I couldn't find any rocks, just gravel nearby. Ah, all that gravel inside of me, the rough edges of resentments and regrets that block me from experiencing God's perfect love for me and for you. Splash!

Once you clear the inside rubble, the Light can get out. Once you release all those blockages, the Light shines through you.

Then you become a Keeper of the Light, a beacon of light for this world that so needs you to shine.

You don't have to search for some grand mission in life. As writer Anne Lamott said, "Lighthouses don't go running all over an island looking for boats to save; they just stand there shining." Simply shine wherever you are, like the bus driver did. Or like my daughter did one average ordinary day heading home from the store.

After leaving the grocery store on a busy day, rushing home to feed her three hungry kids, my daughter Gabrielle saw a woman kneeling on the ground, weeping on a sidewalk behind the store. Was she sick? Was she hurt? Was it a scam? My daughter stopped and asked, "Are you okay?"

The woman told her she was fine. She wasn't. She didn't want to talk, but my daughter offered comfort in her words and by her presence. Gabrielle told her, "Whatever hard thing you're going through, it will get better. We've all had days like this, but it will get better." She stayed with the woman and promised her life would get better, no matter what she was experiencing.

She stayed until the woman stopped crying. She stayed until the woman was calm. She stayed until the woman got on her feet and said, "I'm going to be okay." She stayed long enough to shine her light.

We're all made of light. We're all stardust. Shining our light never diminishes our light. It brightens the whole world around us. A dear friend once told me, the sun always has enough light to go around for everyone. Even on the cloudiest of days, it is still shining as bright as ever.

I love this poem by the Persian poet Hafiz:

Even after all this time, the Sun never says to the Earth,
    "You owe me."
Look what happens with a love like that. It lights the
    whole sky.

Let's collectively shine, especially when the world feels so
dark. Ask yourself that one, burning question: What if *you* were
the light?
    Then shine.
    Just shine.

3

Bravery takes practice.

One birthday my family surprised me with a birthday cake made of words.

My daughter asked my family to describe me, then had a baker inscribe their words in icing all over the sides of a tall cake. What a joy to see how they saw me: *Brave. Warrior. Passionate. Loving. Spiritual. Helpful. Intense. Author. Inspiring. Generous. Fun.*

The best kind of cake you can give a writer is one made of words. Everyone around the table chose one word on the cake and shared how they saw that quality in me. It was a love fest.

Then her husband, James, asked me to choose one of the words and share how I saw that in myself. I chose the word BRAVE, mostly because I've been afraid my whole life.

I used to think that being afraid meant I wasn't brave. Not after I found this quote: "Bravery is being the only one who knows you're afraid." To be brave isn't to have no fear, it's to not let fear stop you from having a joyful, vibrant life, which is what I have. And you don't have to be brave all the time, just when it's needed most.

The key is to stop focusing on the dangers or the fear. Focus solely on what you can and must do and take the next clear step. You will have the courage for that one step, then the next, then the next.

Life constantly gives us opportunities to be brave. Cancer rubbed my nose in fear. That was the scariest year of my life. Every time one fear was conquered, three more popped up to take its place. Fear was my constant companion before, during, and after surgery, chemo, and radiation.

Finally, I confronted them head on. One day I wrote down all my fears so they would stop swirling around inside my head. Within minutes, I had a long list of fears in my journal. I was scared of . . .

Having cancer.

Losing my breast.

Being disfigured from surgery.

Going under anesthesia.

Not waking up from surgery.

Losing both breasts and never feeling like a woman again.

Being scarred and ugly.

Never feeling sexy.

My husband losing interest in me.

Losing all my hair from chemotherapy.

Being too sick to exercise and eat.

Looking pale and sickly and scaring people.

Missing work and losing my job and my house.

The chemo not working.

Having fast-growing cancer.

The cancer spreading.

Being told I have only months to live.

Dying before my daughter married.

Dying before I had grandchildren to spoil.

Getting pitied by everyone.

Getting pitied by no one.

Dying a horrible, long, painful, boring death.

Lingering too long and making everyone miserable.

Once I listed them all, I surrendered them all. I set them all in God's lap, a God who loves me, not my old Catholic school bogeyman God. You can't surrender your life to a God you don't trust. My old image of God, a scary guy in the sky wielding fire and brimstone and keeping score of all my sins, had to go. That God of my misunderstanding was replaced by a God of my understanding, one who is the Source of all light and love and joy. I asked that God to remove whatever fears stood in the way of being useful and fill the huge empty space left with great love.

My friend Brian taught me this: "Instead of telling God how big your problems are, tell your problems how big your God is." It works on fear, too.

I tell my fears what a badass my God is. I'm starting to tell them what a badass I am, too. Cancer made me braver. Even though many of the fears above came true, life was still good.

Self-help guru Louise Hay once said, "Fear is lack of trust in yourself." Whoa. That gave me a jolt. Instead of telling myself, "I'm going to be brave," I tell myself, "I *am* brave."

Now when I'm scared, I call it bravery practice. If I have a dentist appointment, I get to practice being brave. In the elevator, I pose like Superman. In the bathroom, I chest thump like a gorilla. Yep, I got this.

I decided fear is boring. It keeps you in the rut of what is familiar, and you keep carving that groove deeper and deeper. A friend in recovery asked me once, "Do you know the difference between a rut and a grave? There's a little more room to move around." But not much.

When I have to face a challenge that scares me, I reframe it. I tell myself I'm going to Warrior Training School or Bravery Boot Camp. I choose being a warrior over being a worrier. No matter how scary life is, I'm in. All in.

Instead of just taking inventory of my fears, someone suggested I write out my Courage Inventory and create a Bravery Resume. *What's the most courageous thing you've ever done?* I wrote at the top of my list, *I'm so brave that I . . .*

Had a baby at 21 without any painkillers and was my own Lamaze coach, too.

Became an emergency medical technician and gave first aid to victims of accidents, injuries, and illnesses.

Responded to a fire at a propane gas company with propane tanks flying in the air, blowing up all around me.

Picked up dead bodies for a funeral home to pay the rent.

Ended an engagement with a man who cheated on me and didn't leave him for another man. I left him for me.

Went white water rafting three times even though I fell out of the raft and into the river every time.

Learned to drive a stick shift up a giant hill even though the car almost slid all the way back down because I had it in the wrong gear.

Got counseling to heal from child abuse and sexual assaults.

Spoke the truth about the abuse and risked losing people who loved me.

Rode a horse in the desert in Tucson at night with two strangers who carried guns to scare away coyotes.

Forgave my dad and my mom.

Hiked and backpacked in the mountains for a week at Dolly Sods, a federal wilderness area in West Virginia.

Faced cancer head on. I had a lumpectomy, chemotherapy, and radiation.

Showed up for each chemo knowing how sick the last one made me.

Faced the world bald.

Underwent genetic testing and discovered I carried the BRCA1 gene for breast cancer.

Had a double mastectomy and had my ovaries removed.

Decided against breast reconstruction and faced the world flat.

Wrote newspaper columns that challenged the decisions and actions of powerful people, prosecutors, judges, police chiefs, and editors, the very bosses who signed my checks.

Flew to New York City and met a slew of publishers hoping for a book deal.

Completed four book tours in Poland.

Held my head high when I ran into the high school football player decades after he raped me at 17.

Had both lenses in my eyes replaced to remove cataracts and restore my vision to nearly 20/20.

Took a boat ride in Ireland to Skellig Michael, the sacred island featured in the Star Wars movies, *The Force Awakens* and *The Last Jedi.* The sea was so rough that three out of five boats turned back and the lady next to me threw up the whole time.

Climbed all 618 steps alone to the top of Skellig Michael.

Took a doors-off helicopter ride over an active volcano in Hawaii and felt the heat of the Earth churning below me.

Faced life with hope every single day no matter what scared me.

Yes, I have a resume that reminds me I am bigger and stronger and bolder than I often feel. So do you. Those bravery credentials prove that I am more than a survivor. I am a warrior. So are you.

Write down everything you're afraid of, then write your bravery resume. Construct a timeline of courageous acts from childhood, grade school, middle school, high school, college, work, health, relationships, travel, parenting, adventures taken, and problems conquered.

Fear doesn't stand a chance against your bravery credentials.

If you don't believe me, believe these words: "Fate whispers, 'You're not strong enough to withstand the storm.' The warrior whispers back, 'I am the storm.'"

So am I.

So are you.

4

When it comes to going after what you love, don't take no for an answer—especially from yourself.

If you were a bench warmer like me, there is hope.

I've tried out for a lot of sports in my life but was never good at any of them: softball, basketball, volleyball, track. I was what they call a "bench warmer." I sat on the bench, keeping it warm while the better athletes ran around and scored. I rarely played any real time on any field or court.

Over the years, I gave up believing I had it in me to be athletic. Then I met Katie Spotz. She is the queen of endurance challenges and adventures. At 19, she became the youngest person to row alone across the Atlantic Ocean without an engine.

And get this—she was the worst rower in college.

She wasn't always motivated. She, too, was a bench warmer.

When she had to take a one-credit gym class to get her high school diploma, she thought it was a waste of time. She tried to get out of doing it but couldn't, so she took the easiest class, one she knew she could get an A in: walking and running.

"I was forced to take a gym class," she said. "It's funny, the very things we try to avoid can be these divine interventions, these divine moments, the very things that would bring us on a path we would never imagine."

After weeks of walking, she ran. One mile. And hated it. But she knew it was possible to run a mile. She decided to prove herself wrong and have her doubt replaced with curiosity. She discovered that endurance events were the best way to stretch herself. Instead of saying, "I can't," she started saying, "I don't think that's possible, but let's see."

Now, she runs a marathon every week for training. The woman who could barely run a mile completed a 138-mile run. That first marathon was hard. Now it's habit.

"It's muscle memory," she said. "I've already fought the demons of, 'Oh, you're so ridiculous to think you could possibly do this.' I had a lot of that, of those real mental challenges to face before I could even think about the physical challenges. It's like working out a muscle: The repetitive challenges of life make you learn to become better at facing them."

Most times, we're the only ones putting limits on ourselves. It can become a habit that's hard to break.

When people tell her, "I could never run a marathon," she challenges them and asks, "Oh, you've tried? Which one did you try?" Of course they say, I didn't actually try. She says, "Well, that's a requirement. You actually have to try. No one does it without trying."

Of course, you're not going to succeed at something you haven't done.

So why did the worst rower on the college rowing team set out to conquer the Atlantic Ocean? Katie did it with just her arms and her oars, with no spotting boat for company, with no engine for back up.

Something kept tugging at her to do it. She told it, "I don't even know how to row a boat. Why are you bothering me, idea? This doesn't make sense."

The last American to attempt it before her was an Olympic rower, someone much more qualified. It was a ridiculous idea. Katie had student loans to pay. Plus, she didn't want to die. But that tug on her heart wouldn't go away.

"I tried so hard to ignore it, but I knew that I would regret it," she said. "It kept creeping up. The curiosity of it. There are certain experiences in life you can't possibly know until you experienced them. When something is bigger than anything you can imagine, it requires you leaning on God."

She had two options: Row the ocean. Or forever regret not rowing it.

Katie grew up in Mentor, Ohio, a city east of Cleveland, so she trained on Lake Erie. Friends and family had their doubts about her navigating the ocean alone, especially after she had an accident during a trial run on Lake Erie.

She set off anyway, in a bright 19-foot yellow boat with no motor or sail. Katie would rely on just her body, her oars, the wind, and the waves with 3,000 miles ahead of her. The boat already was named Liv, which is Norwegian for *life*.

Katie filled the boat with freeze-dried meals, high-energy drinks, navigation tools, a machine to convert salt water into drinking water, a jet boil stove, charts, an iPod for music, a laptop, satellite phone, two sets of oars, and 3,000 chocolate bars she stored below the water line so they wouldn't melt.

Electricity came from two solar panels on each cabin. The boat weighed 1,000 pounds fully loaded.

She shoved off from Dakar, Senegal, a shipping port in West Africa. There would be no stops before landing in French Guinea in South America, but the ocean had other plans and took her to Guyana.

She used a bucket for a bathroom and kept time like a prisoner, drawing lines on the inside of her boat. She found beauty in the monotony and survived by not making the decision to quit, even when waves hit 20 feet high, barnacles slowed her boat down, and leaking water ruined her stash of candy bars. She endured deadly storms, a fire, sunburn, sleep deprivation, blisters, bruises, a Portuguese man-o-war sting, and those 20-foot-tall waves.

But magic surrounded her, especially at night. "There's no one else, it's all for you," she said. "No pictures could justify the beauty of it. I was constantly in awe of the vastness. We live in a beautiful world with so many places to explore. It's just you and nature and the elements."

The visits by dolphins and sea turtles gave her glimmers of hope just when she needed it. Plankton sparkled like glitter around her boat at night.

At 22 years old, she became the youngest person to row solo across the Atlantic. It took 70 days and 3,038 miles.

She joined the U.S. Coast Guard and lives in Portland, Maine. She still runs a marathon every week. She learned so many life lessons that she wrote a book, *Just Keep Rowing: Lessons from the Atlantic Ocean from the Youngest Person to Row it Alone*. The book is full of 70 lessons, one for every day she spent alone.

Before the ocean, the longest time she had spent alone was 24 hours.

"Being alone, I had a fear about that. As far away as I was, I still felt connected. No matter how far away you go, you can't erase these deep connections to each other. Those don't go away," she said.

"Yes, I had fear, but I could use it to act accordingly. I was so physically exhausted; it was very zombielike. I didn't have the energy to be afraid. I learned that you can keep going even though you're sleep deprived."

She has competed in five Ironman triathlons, cycled across the United States, completed a 325-mile river swim, cycled across New Zealand, ran 100 miles nonstop in under 20 hours, and was the first person to run 138 miles nonstop across Maine in 33 hours, raising funds for a clean water project in Tanzania. Katie also raised over $275,000 for safe drinking water projects around the world.

Reading her website www.katiespotz.com will wear you out. She is an endurance athlete, charitable ambassador, author, and world-record holder. She set a Guinness World Record for the most consecutive days to run an ultramarathon distance. Her Run4Water 341-mile journey began in Cincinnati and finished in Cleveland, Ohio, after running 11 ultra-marathons for 11 days consecutively to fund 11 water projects in Uganda.

Every challenge she does, she does for others.

"If someone else can do it, it means we have a chance, too," she said. "I learn for all what's possible for all of us. We can face things, we can overcome things, we can do things."

She still rarely feels motivated to run a marathon but does it anyway.

"Do it and the motivation kicks in. Motivation comes with movement and action. I'm not a Nike commercial when I wake up in the morning," she said. "I'm not a very motivated person. Motivation sometimes happens *after* you show up, kind of like your late friend to the party."

Find your ocean.

It might be an athletic competition, a work challenge, a travel adventure, or a spiritual mountain to climb.

Once you find your ocean, don't wait for the motivation.

Just start rowing.

Tomorrow isn't guaranteed, so live the hell out of today.

When my cousin was diagnosed with a deadly brain tumor, her husband stood by her side as cancer turned their lives upside down.

Doctors gave her seven months to live. She was just 58 and had two teenage sons.

Nancy underwent surgery, chemotherapy, and radiation, but it could only slow the tumor's growth. She went into remission for nearly three-and-a-half years. When the tumor recurred, she needed something more aggressive and became a medical pioneer.

Her story was spotlighted on the national TV show *60 Minutes* when she agreed to participate in a clinical trial to save her from glioblastoma multiforme, one of the deadliest, most aggressive brain cancers.

Doctors injected a modified version of poliovirus into her brain tumor to kill it. The treatment gave Nancy and her husband, Greg Justice, just 18 more months together before a massive inflammation in her brain killed her.

She died on April 6, 2016. She was 60.

Two months later, her husband Greg was diagnosed with lung cancer.

Stage IV non-small cell lung cancer. He never smoked a day in his life. Only four people out of one hundred last five years with that diagnosis.

He watched her die. Now it was his turn. At least that's what people thought.

Then Greg did something wild and daring. He tossed out his old life and started living a brand new one. He took medical disability and retired from his job of 30 years.

He traveled the world.

He fell in love with life and with a beautiful soul named Mary.

He's still very much alive. Cancer gave him an expiration date he refuses to honor.

Greg didn't waste any time on pity parties. He did the treatment to fight cancer. He underwent chemotherapy and then had radiation, but the cancer came back.

He was already living the hell out of life but hit the gas pedal even harder to enjoy the time he had left. Their two sons were in college, and, at the time, he had enough money, so he retired and traveled the world. He started writing. He fell in love. He got married.

Married!

And as I write this, he is still alive. Very much alive.

How do you squeeze more life out of the life you have left?

He used these five coping strategies:

1. Face the brutal facts but never lose hope.

2. Know that God is in control.

3. Take one day at a time.

4. Live every day to the fullest.

5. Count your blessings.

You decide that today, this day, you are very much alive. You stay grateful for what you do have. You accept that much of it will feel messy and horrible, but there will still be magic and beauty scattered everywhere.

You live the hell out of the day you are in.

That's how he got through Nancy's cancer. That's how he got through his.

He shared her journey with me to help others, because her journey with cancer helped him face his.

Before Nancy's diagnosis, Greg was a boat builder running a plant for Regal Marine Industries in Valdosta, Georgia. The company made luxury performance boats, and he was director of manufacturing with 219 employees. When the economy tanked, they went down to 60 employees, and he worried they might have to shut down.

Then his wife got cancer.

They were intense years, but good years, in which they made the most of their life together.

"She was so brave. She never complained," Greg said.

Nancy was such a gentle, quiet soul. The only reason she stood out in a room was because she had bright red hair and such a quiet, calm demeanor that never seemed to waver.

"When you get a horrible diagnosis, life is not over," Greg told me. "For us, the best part was just beginning. We had had a good life up until then, but I wasn't living to the fullest. I learned how to love expecting nothing back. One of my biggest thrills was Nancy looking in my eyes and telling me, 'I never realized how much you loved me.' To tell you the truth, I didn't either!

"What it all boils down to? It's about love," he said. "Nancy and I had no idea the gold mine we were sitting on. You can very easily dwell on the bad stuff: My job was difficult, my wife had cancer, she passed away, I had heart surgery, then stage IV lung cancer, but there was beauty sprinkled all through that.

"I look back on that time. I wouldn't choose to do it again, but what I've learned and where it's brought me today, I wouldn't trade it for anything. We were loved! We knew we had good friends, but man, the love we had.

"God was right there with us the whole time. I call it the beautiful, horrible journey. Parts of it were horrible, but man, the way we loved. And the way we were loved."

He knows God has been with him through his diagnosis.

"God is good all the time. People need to know you can still live the hell out of life even in the face of a horrible diagnosis," he said.

He also knows that no matter how good the medical scan results are, he's living on borrowed time. His doctor urged him, "If you want to do something with your boys, you better do it now." So he talked to his boss, who encouraged him to quit to spend time with his sons, who were both in college.

Too many people sleepwalk through life. Cancer wakes you up. He jumped into life and took his sons on a long vacation out West.

But they needed to go on living their own lives. He wanted to find companionship, not romance, so his sister set him up to meet her friend, Mary.

"I wanted companionship," he said. "I wasn't looking for a great love affair, just someone to have dinner with."

He was brutally honest with Mary about his diagnosis and

said he just wanted a female friend. Mary told him she wanted more.

"God has promised me a husband," she said, "and I don't want to waste my time. You're not for me."

He laughs about it now. "Wow, shot down by God!"

Still, they met for coffee at Disney Springs. "We had the best first date in the history of the world," he said.

As they were standing in line waiting to be seated, she moved to the Latin music so fluidly and easily and alluringly to him. Then they danced to some upbeat country music at a venue by the lake. It was as if they were in a world all their own. No one else and nothing else existed.

They fell in love, but he had her talk to a counselor at the cancer center and to his oncologist so she knew what she was getting into. They also went through counseling with his two sons and went into the new marriage with eyes wide open.

"I haven't done anything to deserve so much I've been blessed with," he said. "It's a reminder, man, God loves us. A horrible diagnosis is not the end. It's a wake-up call to live life to the fullest."

A life he is still busy living.

6

Everything changes. Let it.

My daughter was enjoying a snack outside a nearby coffee shop one sunny July day with her youngest child when they saw the smoke.

A mile away, Fernway was on fire.

Fernway.

That's what everyone called her children's elementary school in Shaker Heights, Ohio. That's what they call her neighborhood. Fernway. That's what hundreds of families call home. The school is nestled in a neighborhood where families gather after school and on weekends to support and celebrate each other.

Word spread faster than the flames and smoke: "Fernway is on fire!"

Jaws dropped. Hearts sank. Tears flowed.

News reports said, "No one was hurt in the fire."

No one was physically hurt, but the entire neighborhood was devastated.

The roof of Fernway Elementary School caught fire on July 10, 2018, as roofers were repairing it. The small staff inside at the time was safely evacuated. It took crews from 20 different fire departments nearly five hours to put out the fire. It took over 300,000 gallons of water, draining the local water tower.

When my daughter texted me the photo of the smoke and told me of the fire, my heart sank, too. My three grandchildren attended Fernway, which runs from kindergarten to fourth grade. The youngest had just registered for kindergarten; the older ones were in second and fourth grade. That coming fall would have been the only time in their entire lives that all three siblings would be enrolled at the same school.

I drove over and watched as firefighters climbed up the ladders, sweating in the hot sun as water poured out of the building in rivers down the sidewalk and smoke billowed out the top.

The entire roof had collapsed.

Every teacher lost all their supplies they had collected and used year after year. Every library book, gone. Every desk, gone. Every pencil, art supply, musical instrument, gone. Either the fire or the water ruined them forever.

Police surrounded the building with yellow tape. The community surrounded it with love, drawing chalk hearts and messages of thanks, hope, and love. Down the front steps in giant letters, they wrote a single message on each step:

THANK YOU

FIREFIGHTERS

POLICE

SHAKER

The fire was ruled an accident. Workers had been repairing the roof, which was part wood and part slate. They had been using a heating element in an asphalt area when the wood caught fire.

It broke my heart every time I drove past the school. It

looked like a gaping wound. No one knew when or if it would be fixed. The school was built in 1927. Would they even bother to rebuild it?

My daughter loves her Fernway neighborhood. So many people live online these days, it's rare to see neighborhoods with kids outside. Every day looks like a block party on her street, there are so many kids out playing soccer, football, or riding bikes. On her block alone, I counted 33 kids. She said if you go from corner to corner, there are at least 55.

People grieved on Facebook. They called Fernway "a little slice of paradise . . . a neighborhood of hope, joy, and resilience."

My daughter wrote:

> Today I am reminded how much I love our community. While sitting at a coffee shop, I watched as area fire departments zipped past us, sirens blaring, black smoke filling the sky. We talked about teamwork and paused to wish them well. We learned later that nearly 20 municipalities came to help—talk about teamwork!
>
> The streets were filled with people as if it were a block party. I felt as though gathering lessened the loss a tiny bit. I learned neighbors delivered water bottles, bananas, and Popsicles to the firefighters and opened their doors.

She posted pictures from the last day of school, thank-you notes the kids organized, and an image of the school standing tall.

Later, she and her husband, James, took the children to the school after dinner. The community set up a gratitude station with poster board and markers so kids and parents could write notes to the first responders and helpers. A Girl Scout troop provided chalk. Students from 65 years ago wrote messages of thanks.

So many diverse generations of families had shared traditions that made them one family, the Fernway Family: The Halloween parade of costumes around the building, the infamous Clap Outs for all graduating fourth graders, and the stream of graduating high school seniors who return every year to thank the school.

On the last day of school at Fernway, all the students surround the flag and sing, "You're a grand old flag . . . " as they lower the stars and stripes. They also belt out the Fernway school song, "F-E-R-N-W-A-Y Fernway is the best!"

It still is.

The kids didn't know where they would go to school in the fall, but the principal promised them, wherever they go, they would still be Fernway students.

#FernwayForever wasn't just a hashtag to them.

It was a flameproof mantra.

The school district had to relocate 315 students. Three other schools made room for them, but it was hard being the "new" kid and losing your own teachers and friends. Most kids walked to school; now most of them would have to take a bus.

The upside? The Fernway kids met children from the other schools, rode in a bus, and ate in a lunchroom instead of classrooms—all new experiences.

Still, it was hard to see that abandoned shell wrapped in yellow police tape. Gradually, we saw construction crews rebuild it, week after week, month after month.

For two years, the children were scattered at different schools, but they always called themselves Fernway students. When my grandson Asher graduated from fourth grade, even though he wasn't in the building, he and his class came back to hold their graduation ceremony outside near the fenced-off construction site.

The principal gave all the kids plastic yellow hard hats. The fire department sent a big ladder truck and hoisted up a giant American flag. Each child got special gift: a piece of slate wrapped in tissue paper, a piece of the roof from the old school.

The neighborhood organized, attended school board meetings, and advocated for modern upgrades like air conditioning and a bigger play space.

When they finally reopened Fernway for the 2020–21 school year, people oohed and ahhed. They call it Fernway 2.0. It took $17.5 million to rebuild it. It's better than before. The new Fernway has air conditioning, something rarely found in their school district. It has a big multipurpose room for lunch, so the kids don't have to eat at their desks anymore.

The library became a state-of-the-art learning center with a place for kids to do more science, technology, engineering, arts, and mathematics projects together.

There's a speech and occupational therapy room. An elevator to make the school handicapped accessible. All new furniture. An updated music and art room.

Every room has high-tech lighting systems. The playground was recreated with nature play areas, bike racks, tables, benches, and much more green space.

Every single thing inside is brand new.

When my youngest grandchild finished third grade, her first

year at the new school, I went to the big last day of school cel-
ebration on the lawn. As they took down the flag for summer,
the principal announced the school was going to get a mascot.

A bird.

A phoenix, a mythical bird that rose out of the ashes.

Everyone cheered. And some of us cried.

7

If it was supposed to be different, it would be.

The writer and monk Thomas Merton wrote that he wished to "disappear into the writing, perhaps it could be a prayer." That's what my brother-in-law Tom's writing—and his life— were: a prayer.

Tom Raithel's great love was poetry. His wife, my sister Therese, called it his "magnificent obsession."

I think it was also his church.

Words are so holy that in the Bible, the book of John starts with this sentence: "In the beginning was the Word, and the Word was with God, and the Word was God."

Tom practiced the sacrament of writing known to the world as poetry. He loved words and weighed each one with his pen and that brilliant mind of his and that deep heart of his. Each word had to land just the right way on the reader's heart.

And it did.

Tom didn't see clouds, he saw "sailboats of gods, climbing and crossing waves of sky; the misty breath of giants / snoring under the rocks and forests, / shaking the world in their sleep."

He saw "flying islands . . . mirrors of thought, lakes in the sky, / modeling clay for cherubs and angels, airliners filled with traveling dreams."

It was hard to get past the irony of the title of his last book, *This Easy Falling*. Or maybe not.

The saint Julian of Norwich once said, "First the fall, and then the recovery from the fall. Both are the mercy of God."

Both. Yes, both.

Tom went to Milwaukee to enjoy a weekend with friends and never saw the inside of his home again. But his home was always in words.

He slipped in a hotel shower and broke his neck, leaving him a quadriplegic. Even after the fall that paralyzed him, his words were of gratitude.

He told his wife, "My faith has never been stronger."

He had the most peaceful look on his face when he told me in Cleveland's MetroHealth Rehabilitation Institute: "I've had a really good life. I'm really at peace. I don't feel I've been cheated at all."

Tom smiled when he took account of what remained: "I have good friendships and family. I'm 71. I have had a pretty full life."

His new book had not yet come out, so I became his assistant to do the final edits. Tom was such a good writer that I found just one random comma, like a fallen eyelash on the top of a page. Tom had already measured every single word like it mattered—because each one did to him.

Tom lived to see his book of poetry published. He had the biggest book event of his life at the nursing home. With that, he completed his life. He loved his wife, his brothers, his extended family, and his chosen family, dear friends from childhood and from recovery.

Tom never seemed upset to see a bracelet on his body that read NO CPR. He had embraced life all along. Poetry did that to him, for him.

In all the times we sat in the courtyard at the nursing home, there was no striving for more. He would tilt back his wheelchair and bask in the sun, savoring every ray like it might be his last. He knew.

There's a saying in recovery: "If the only time you're talking to God is when you're in trouble . . . you're in trouble." Tom was never in trouble, even after he fell, because he had a deep spiritual life.

His response to every challenge was almost always a quiet surrender followed by deep gratitude for what he had, not regret over what he had lost.

Think about that: He drove out to spend a weekend with friends and never returned to the life he created here. He lost his ability to move, to shave himself, to bathe himself, to use a bathroom, to feed himself, to open a book, to go to a baseball game, to drive a car, to play guitar, to get on a plane and see the rest of the world.

In those early days, hope was a moving target. His world became call buttons and catheters, splints and gloves, PT and OT, speech therapy and art therapy, then swelling, spasms, and pain.

And yet, his words? Gratitude.

Tom constantly told those who helped him, "You guys are

amazing." I sat with him nearly weekly and never once, never once in 18 months, did he ask, "Why me?" Or ask, "Will I ever be able to . . . " (fill in the blank).

He let the blanks remain blank. Poets know when to be silent.

His silence challenged us all to grow out of the shock and anger and fear. He helped us expand our prayer lives and challenged our ideas of God and mercy and hope.

He helped us grow closer as a family as we all navigated which hospital, which surgery, which rehab, which nursing home. As we sorted out legal and financial and medical issues. As we fretted over which bed to buy, which wheelchair to purchase, which voice recognition software could help him use the TV, the lights, the phone.

All Tom wanted? Those precious moments when we read aloud to him, watched a ballgame, prayed together, called to catch up, shared a laugh, a story, or a meeting on Zoom.

In Tom's beloved A.A. fellowship, they often say, "Don't quit before the miracle happens." We didn't get the miracle we all wanted, but we witnessed so many miracle moments, how could we feel shortchanged if Tom didn't? Like when he brushed his teeth for the first time after the fall, and fed himself, and drove the wheelchair, and created a piece of art in therapy as a gift for his wife.

Christians might call Tom's injury a cross to bear. If that's true, it's one we all took turns carrying for a while, one Therese rarely put down.

Or maybe Tom carried us. He showed us how to love the smallness of it all: a song in the Piazza at the nursing home, a scoop of chocolate ice cream, a breeze kissing his face.

Tom recovered from the fall, but not the way any of us wanted him to. We had hoped he would return to writing. I offered to be his assistant and told him I would type out the words for him. He just smiled. He knew the poetry had to flow directly from his head, heart, and hands to the page.

I still miss so much about Tom. He came over weekly to walk our dog and always brought his own treats and potty bags. He taught me and my grandson to keep the score at a baseball game by pencil. It forces you to savor every play. We learned the fine art of penciling in a backwards K for those strikeouts where the batter didn't even swing. We called ourselves the Geek Squad. When my grandkids, Asher, Ainsley, and River, made homemade Christmas tree decorations and brought over a small tree, Tom kept it up all year—with the lights on.

I'll never forget when River brought poems her fourth-grade class wrote for Tom. After she read each one by his bedside, Tom took time to praise them all.

Many shared the great gift of recovery in meetings with Tom almost every Saturday on Zoom. I'll never forget the moment the secretary of the meeting asked, "Is anyone willing to sponsor?" Tom always wanted to be of service, so from the wheelchair in his bedroom, he lifted his hand.

We didn't even know he could lift his hand until that moment.

It's comforting to believe that Tom completed his life. In his 41 years of sobriety, he received every single one of the 12 promises offered by A.A., including these:

We are going to know a new freedom and a new happiness.

We will not regret the past nor wish to shut the door on it.

We will comprehend the word serenity and we will know peace.

No matter how far down the scale we have gone, we will see how our experience can benefit others.

We will intuitively know how to handle situations which used to baffle us.

We will suddenly realize that God is doing for us what we could not do for ourselves.

Tom made his life a poem and a prayer. One that will bless our lives forever.

8

Cry like you mean it.

Grief needs an exit ramp.

If it doesn't get one, it will carve a path like a wild tornado through you with nowhere to go.

I love this quote by author Jamie Anderson: "Grief, I've learned, is really just love. It's all the love you want to give but cannot. All that unspent love gathers up in the corners of your eyes, the lump in your throat, and in that hollow part of your chest. Grief is just love with no place to go."

Writing is my way to give grief an exit. Crying and talking to others also help me release it.

After my beautiful nephew, Michael, died unexpectedly at 34, the grief of losing him just thrashed me around like wild ocean waves. The gentle waves I could handle, but some days, it felt like a tsunami let loose and swept me away.

My friend in Arizona shared a beautiful message on Facebook after her daughter died unexpectedly at 24. Nigerian poet Ijeoma Umebinyuo offered three steps to healing: "You must let the pain visit. You must allow it to teach you. You must not allow it to overstay."

I needed to hear about all three.

Another friend who lost her teenage brother to suicide when she was just eight is a pillar of support in my life. I called her when I was drowning in tears over my nephew. I loved him so much. She said it's okay to climb in the highchair and throw a fit like a baby and rant and be angry and sad and cry and let it rip. You just don't stay in the highchair forever. At some point, you climb back into life.

Instead of giving yourself a "time out" like we do children, you give yourself a "time in" to nurture yourself so you can feel all the pain. That way it can go all the way through you and be done. Maybe not done forever, but done for today, done for this wave.

People often say, You need to have a good cry.

What is a good cry?

Is there really such a thing as a bad cry?

There is. A bad cry is when you need to cry and don't. A bad cry is when you try to hold in big tears and suck them back down those tiny tear ducts and clog them up for days. A bad cry is when you start to cry and put your head down so no one sees. A bad cry is when you judge yourself too harshly for feeling so deeply.

Tears need to get out. They are like Windex for the soul. I even cry at TV commercials, especially during the Olympics. Tears flush out pain, sadness, and grief. They allow others to see you vulnerable and human. Your tears give them permission to cry.

How powerful that humans are the only animal that cries for emotional reasons. And that the shortest line in the Bible is, "Jesus wept." Not cried. Wept.

What's a good cry?

No apologies and lots of tissue. A snotty nose. Your face hurts when you're done. Your eyes are red and swollen. You feel raw and hollow and empty. And you are. Emptied from some of that pain you had swallowed that needed to be released.

As I wrote in *God Never Blinks,* it's better to cry with someone than to cry alone. But when I find myself alone, certain songs help my tears find the exit ramp: "Hallelujah," by Jeff Buckley, which we sang at my nephew's funeral. "The Dance," by Garth Brooks. "Bless the Broken Road," by Rascal Flatts. "The House That Built Me," by Miranda Lambert. *When I Get Where I'm Going*, by Brad Paisley and Dolly Parton.

Or you can read a book that helps you cry: *The Fault in Our Stars*, by John Green. *My Sister's Keeper*, by Jodi Picault. *Cry, the Beloved Country,* by Alan Paton. *Dear Edward*, by Anna Napolitano. *Wonder*, by R. J. Palacio. *The Book Thief,* by Markus Zusak, or the last Harry Potter book by J. K. Rowling.

Or watch a movie, like *Stepmom, Up, Titanic, Beaches, Steel Magnolias, The Color Purple, Dead Poets Society, If Beale Street Could Talk*, or *Encanto*.

They say, "big girls don't cry." Yes, we do.

Crying is in my DNA.

The Irish don't just cry, we wail. We have a name for it: keening. It's a spiritual way to sing the soul home. It's a wordless cry, a plea, a vocal, poetic lament for the dead, a musical expression of grief, a wild, holy, raw cry from the depths of your soul to free your soul. They call it an Irish howl.

In the Gaelic Celtic tradition, you perform intense, wordless wailing at the graveside of someone you loved. They once had professional mourners who were paid with whiskey to keen. They would sing and chant all night long.

Then the Catholic Church called it a pagan practice and tried to outlaw it. Priests didn't want to have people feeling so deeply, loudly, and openly. They tried to banish the keeners, threatening excommunication.

In time, others let go of keening because they saw it as old fashioned, backward, and primitive. It is primal, but in a good way, a clean, powerful, natural way.

Ask anyone who has worked in a hospital where children die. There is a grief that can only be let out in a wail, a wordless howl of pain, when you lose a child.

Instead of shoving grief down, or drinking it away and drugging yourself numb, have a good cry. Put your whole body into it. Clap. Rock. Sway. Beat your chest, pound your fists, stomp your feet, stand on the Earth, look to the heavens, and let it rip. Let loose a terrible wail. Sound your barbaric yawp.

I love these words from poet Walt Whitman: "I sound my barbaric yawp over the roofs of the world."

What is a yawp?

A loud cry, yell, or wail.

So wail. Cry. Scream.

Consider this your permission slip to cry. The more you loved, the bigger the grief, the louder and longer the cry.

Give that pain room to pass through you, all the way through, and out.

And when it does pass through, it will leave you raw and hollowed and ready to receive even more love.

9

If you only got what you wanted, you would sell yourself short.

Like any new dad, Rob Snow couldn't wait to show off his beautiful new baby boy.

But when people realized that his son, Henry, had Down syndrome, their faces fell, and they said the words Rob and his wife, Ellen, came to dread: "I'm so sorry."

The look of sadness and sympathy on their faces made him want to scream. Instead, he wrote a book, *What I Should Have Said*.

Rob, who lives in Medina, Ohio, says the book is no Pulitzer Prize winner. He calls it a "bathroom book." It's a slim 89 pages packed with humor, sarcasm, wit, and wisdom. (It's available on his website www.standupfordowns.org.)

He wrote it for people in the Down syndrome community who constantly hear the ignorant comments. He wrote it to raise awareness about what Down syndrome is and isn't.

We are not sad and we don't go to bed crying every night, he writes.

"What we are is a part of a very special club that understands this unique and beautiful side of life. We get to watch our children, relatives, or friends with special needs overcome or work through obstacles, appreciate the things in life we've never considered, hit milestones, and stay more positive than any group I've ever encountered."

Sounds like a gift to me. That's what Henry is. A gift. That's what every child is. A gift.

If you knew that, you wouldn't say things like...

I'm so sorry. Please don't be. Henry has taught Rob and Ellen more about life than any parents could hope for.

When life gives you lemons, make lemonade. When Rob hears that, he wants to say, "Did you just call my son a lemon?"

Didn't your doctor offer you amniocentesis? That one makes Rob want to say, "Yep, they sure did. I just had this crazy idea that even if my child had some sort of disability, he might still have some value in this world."

Weren't you so disappointed when you found out? Rob's response is, "Yes. Can't deny it. And every day he reminds me how wrong I was to think that."

What a terrible disease. It's not a disease, it's a condition. The National Down Syndrome Society describes it this way: "Typically, the nucleus of each cell contains 23 pairs of chromosomes. Down syndrome occurs when an individual has a full or partial extra copy of chromosome 21."

Do you just cry every night? I love his response: "Only when I think about how badly misinformed people are about my son."

You've got to laugh at some people. Like the one who said, "He doesn't look so downsy." Rob's response? "Oh, he must not have it today."

Rob sums up the heart of his life in two sentences: "I have a son with Down syndrome and a love of comedy. . . The rest of my life has been a merger of those two things."

Laughter is what Rob does best. He's the founder of Stand Up for Downs. He also does a comedy show called "We Need A Sign," addressing the common experiences parents share raising a child with special needs. His mission is to improve the lives of people with Down syndrome.

Rob grew up near Cleveland, Ohio, and always had a passion for comedy. He obsessively watched it on TV in all its forms and, of course, was the class clown. He later studied improv at the famous Second City theatre in Chicago. Then he started performing stand-up on stages throughout the country.

But in 2000, he hung up his comedy dreams to pursue the "normal life": wife, children, picket fence—you know, stability. Everything was going according to plan until 2009. He and Ellen had a son, Charlie, and decided to have another child. Everything changed when Henry was born with Down syndrome.

Rob's book is an eye opener. His humor is a heart opener. His own heart was cracked wide open the day Henry was born.

When Ellen was pregnant, there were a few soft markers on the ultrasound that might indicate Down syndrome, but they were dismissed. When Henry was born, "We saw this gorgeous little boy," Rob said.

The doctor said he didn't see any Down syndrome traits and was about 90 percent sure, but they did a blood test. A few hours later, a pediatrician they had randomly chosen came in the room and said, "Well, I'm about 80 percent sure your son has Down syndrome."

Rob's heart fell into his stomach. At that moment, it felt like the worst news to hear. Then the pediatrician said, "And that is awesome," and opened up her laptop and showed them pictures of her daughter. Seeing that five-year-old girl with Down syndrome in pigtails playing soccer gave him a glimpse of the gifts ahead.

What helped him most? He shared these tips:

A problem can actually be a privilege once you embrace it. Educate yourself about what you're up against. Don't believe everything you read on the internet.

Ask for help and accept it. People want to give it, so take it. People feel honored when you receive their help.

Keep finding the positive. It might evaporate now and then, but keep looking for it.

Remember your "why" to stay focused and positive. "When you have your why, every step is easier. Your 'why' is the thing that burns inside of you, that motivates you," he said. "Every time you don't accept help, go back to your 'why.' How committed to it are you?"

Henry inspired Rob to create three one-man shows and the charity Stand Up For Downs. He also inspired The Improvaneers, the only all-Down Syndrome improv group of its kind. Rob started it to help Henry have a better life, to gain skills like problem solving, adapting to change, teamwork, listening, focus, eye contact, and voice projection. All those skills will help Henry socialize at work, at school, and in every relationship.

The classes have changed so many lives. One boy who had both autism and Down syndrome could only say a few words until he took Rob's class. Now he speaks in full sentences and greets friends and family with enthusiasm when they show up at his house.

That first class, Rob chose 10 out of 25 who tried out. Then he trained them for a year and a half once a week. They put on two sold-out shows. They have since booked shows around the country.

When Covid hit, they took the workshops and classes online using Zoom. They got up to 30 classes a week with more than 400 different participants. Rob is also writing a book about how to minimize the mountain.

"Our mountain was Down syndrome," he said. It was also job loss and the death of a dear friend. But loving Henry has prepared him for everything.

"Henry is an absolute, amazing joy," Rob said. "He continues to make me laugh. It's the greatest thing to have him in my life."

When people ask, "Does he know he is different?"

Different? Rob smiles and tells them, "We all are. That's kind of the beauty of it? Right?"

It sure is.

10

God is rarely early, but God is never too late.

Even though we weren't ready, Mom's brain was.

Even though she had 11 children, none of us could give her the kind of daily care she needed and would need more of as this disease progressed.

Most people think Alzheimer's means a person loses their memory. That's only part of it. It creates holes and gaps in a brain.

Mom would see a dozen bright red apples in her fridge and still write "red apples" on her grocery list, as if she needed to buy more. Her brain didn't recognize what was right in front of her. Forgetfulness and memory loss are *consequences* of Alzheimer's disease; they aren't what was actually wrong with her. The disease was like a computer virus attacking Mom's information files, deleting decades of stored data she depended on to live, think, and function.

It's a hard diagnosis to accept. We didn't want Mom to go into a care unit, but also didn't want her to spend her days alone like a shut-in. Crocheting was her one and only stimulation.

Sometimes we saw a clean, funny, witty woman dressed in

church-going clothes whose house was tidy and fridge was full, a woman who could order from a menu, converse with strangers, and remember what she did and didn't need.

Other times we saw her fading away. We saw a woman asking the same questions over and over, who no longer bathed but washed in the sink, who changed the subject when she couldn't remember the topic, who forgot the names of her grandkids and confused the names of her children.

No medicine would fix this or slow it down. Mom tried one drug but didn't like the side effects. This is the best she would ever be.

Ever.

Alzheimer's made it unsafe for her to live alone. We were worried about her forgetting her medicine, falling down the basement steps, or leaving the stove on and burning down her house.

The isolation of living alone didn't help her memory. She deserved better than this. She needed safe surroundings and a better daily quality of life. We didn't want her to endure another lonely, cold Ohio winter as a shut-in. Moving in with one of her children wasn't an option. No one could stay home all day to watch her. Our first floor didn't have a bedroom or a full bathroom.

There were financial decisions to make. She could no longer pay bills or do her own banking. She added an extra zero to a deposit. She tossed bills aside with piles of catalogs. We also needed to keep her safe financially from people who came to the door selling things or asking for donations. She was the perfect target: a forgetful old woman living alone with a checkbook and a heart willing to help strangers.

The toughest part was finding Mom an assisted living place that offered memory care. At some point she would need a locked unit, but we wanted her to have access to the outdoors, to feel the sun, feed the birds, and watch the squirrels. We wanted the best quality of life, access to an outdoor patio, planned activities, personal care, a delicate mix of privacy and independence, yet round the clock care if needed. We wanted someone to help her shower and shampoo, but also wanted to preserve her independence.

She fell into a huge crack: She wasn't ready for a nursing home but wasn't independent enough for independent living.

I called 10 nursing facilities near Mom's small town. There was no suitable memory unit in the area. They were either skilled nursing homes where she would share a bedroom or they were assisted living facilities without a memory care unit. She didn't qualify for a nursing home. She had never been hospitalized. It isn't easy to find assisted living for someone with Alzheimer's that wasn't a nursing home. Mom was in great health—other than Alzheimer's chomping away at her brain.

We wanted a place that felt like home but knew that no place would ever feel like home to her. We all wanted the best for Mom. Unfortunately, it wasn't clear what that was. It also might mean something different to each sibling from our unique perspectives. We kept reminding each other: *We are all doing the best we can with what we have*. It's a moving target, one that might change from week to week.

She kept telling us, "I'm ready to go. I don't know what God is waiting for." She truly was ready to let go of her grip on this life. When I asked her what might be holding her back, she said, "Nothing. I'm ready to go."

After a month of making calls and visiting nursing home options, I was ready to give up. Some people say we're not supposed to pray for a sign, but when I'm feeling really lost or heartsick or hopeless, I beg for one. I pray my Prayer of Desperation, the one where I say bluntly to God, "God, I need Your clarity. If You already gave me an answer, I missed it. Speak louder. Be more obvious. Give me a spotlight, a billboard, or a sledgehammer."

I got all three.

The next day I bumped into a friend of mine, a retired priest. Patrick was a gentle soul who always said the right thing, so I poured my heart out to him.

"Did you try a Catholic home?" he asked.

I never even thought of that.

Being Catholic was my mom's core identity. She was the sacristan at Immaculate Conception Church in Ravenna for 30 years. Before she retired, she helped buy a statue for the church. She saved up her small salary to help pay for the Holy Family statue. Mom was big on the Holy Family, Jesus, Mary, and Joseph. Not so much on baby Jesus. Of course she loved babies. Allegedly. She had 11. She said people shouldn't leave Jesus in the manger after Christmas to die of neglect.

She couldn't afford the whole thing, so she paid for Jesus. Not Jesus the baby, but Jesus the boy. She wanted a statue that depicted him as a boy, so she bought him. She never told us how much it cost. It was between her and God. When they installed that big statue, we took pictures of her standing next to it. She was so proud to see the Holy Family all together, as if she herself had reunited them.

So I started making calls. Each person led me to another

person who finally led me to Light of Hearts Villa in Bedford, Ohio, just 25 minutes from my house. It's a place I had never heard of and would never have found on my own. It wasn't listed on the government website since it was affiliated with Regina Health Center, a nursing home.

Now there's a sign. Regina was looking for a home and found one under the name Regina.

I pulled up to Light of Hearts Villa, and right there in the parking lot stood a huge, almost life-sized white statue of the Holy Family. I nearly crashed right into it. It didn't depict Jesus as a baby but as a boy, just like Mom wanted.

Then I walked inside and saw an entire wall of angel statues, hundreds of them in all shapes and sizes. They fill the old trophy cases left from when Light of Hearts was a high school.

Then God upped the ante. I met Sister Regina.

I kid you not.

A tall, thin, plainclothes nun walked up and introduced herself. "Hi, I'm Sister Regina." She not only had my name, she had the same birthday as Mom.

Now God was just showing off.

Statue? *Check*. Angels? *Check*. Nun with my name? *Check*.

Then a woman named Sister Helen came up to me and said she couldn't wait to meet "that mother of 11" to give her a hug. Sister Helen ran the "Cozy Corner," a little thrift store where people donated things they don't want or things they crotchet. They also crocheted for the poor. Sister Estelle ran the crotchet club that met every Tuesday. These were Mom's kind of people.

This place was like Heaven's Waiting Room.

It was a Catholic assisted-living community run by the Sisters of Charity Cincinnati / Sisters of Charity St. Augustine. The building was once an all-girls Catholic high school. It was built in 1963, closed in 1987, and reopened in 1989 as Light of Hearts Villa for assisted living. They added a locked Alzheimer's unit with apartment-style living. The halls were super wide for class exchange, so they easily fit three wheelchairs in case we wanted to have races down the halls.

They had a bell choir, housekeeping, laundry, meals, and bingo. They had pull cords for help in every room, safety rails everywhere, and staff visits every hour. They had a gorgeous chapel, Mass six days a week, and the rosary every day. Mom would feel like she was already in heaven.

And best of all, they had an opening.

My brother made her business cards with her new address and these words: *Mother of eleven waiting on heaven.*

Waiting for God to take her home on His timetable, not hers.

11

Just when you think you've lost all hope, hope finds you.

We finished the last dinner at the cabin, lit the campfire, and were all set to play a round of flashlight tag to celebrate our last night at Lake Hope.

After spending a relaxing weekend there last year with my brother and his wife, I reserved two cabins for my family to spend time together.

We booked two cabins in southern Ohio for three days in June at Lake Hope State Park, which sits in the Zaleski State Forest, a few hours south of our home in Cleveland. There was no cell service, rare and random internet but endless trees, sky, and fresh air. It felt so good to be free from Facebook and email.

I went with my husband, our daughter, her husband and three kids, and our oldest son, his girlfriend, and her niece. We loved the lake. The kids were exhausted from swimming, paddle boarding, and hiking all day.

Everything went smoothly until a buzz of panic filled the air late Saturday evening. There would be no flashlight tag.

A man in a nearby cabin heard a woman screaming and things being thrown, including her children. He ran to the dining lodge up the hill where there is sketchy cell phone service and somehow managed to reach the rangers to tell them, "This mother is trying to kill her kids!"

Moments later, people huddled outside the cabin next door. Two children had already fled and ran to a stranger's cabin begging for help.

"Our mom is going to kill us!" they cried.

Their mother had been drinking all day and turned violent when she drank. The children had called the emergency number for help four times, but the calls never went through because of the remoteness of the area.

As we tried to sort out what had happened, I walked the mom away from the kids and tried to keep her occupied until the rangers arrived. She stumbled and staggered and rambled incoherently that everything was fine. She looked disheveled, her dress askew. She wasn't any bigger than me, but alcohol can make a person feel and act ten feet tall and bulletproof.

Meanwhile, strangers swooped in to help the boy and girl, giving them food. Everyone asked how they could help. The rangers showed up, led the mom away in handcuffs, and had her sit in their car while they sorted out what to do with the kids. There was talk of a boyfriend who had been staying with her, but he left because of her drinking.

Oh, and he took his gun with him.

Whew. Thank goodness for that.

I tried to talk to the boy, who was nine, and the girl, who was seven. They both had bright yellow hair and bright blue eyes freshly washed from tears of terror and relief.

The girl had fled in her nightie and was barefoot. The boy shivered in shorts in the chilly night air. They looked so vulnerable and scared. We gave them warm clothes and comforting words. My husband kept our kids entertained inside our own cabin while our son guarded the door outside from any other chaos that might erupt.

My daughter and I listened as the details poured out of the two children:

"She grabbed my hair and lifted me up. I was dangling by my hair," the girl said.

The boy shook when he talked about his mom hitting him and throwing fireplace tools at them. He lifted his shirt so the ranger could take a photo of the four-inch scratch on his torso.

She hits us all the time when she's had too much to drink, they said. *We tried to call for help, but it didn't work,* he said. So they fled.

With little cell service and phones with passwords the kids didn't know, it took hours for the rangers to find a next of kin that could come get them. Meanwhile, strangers swooped in to help. The people whose cabin they had fled to had created a temporary refuge for those kids and let them stay for hours.

My daughter and I told them how brave they were to speak up and to flee to get help. We told them they didn't cause their mom's drinking, and they couldn't control it. We also told them their words are the most powerful tools they have.

We grabbed an Uno card game and fed them peanut butter sandwiches and cheese sticks. They won every round. We played cards until the people whose cabin it was needed to get their own kids to bed.

The ranger was going to take the two children to the nearby

dining lodge on the hill to sleep on a couch. The place was dark and deserted. It was almost midnight. The boy looked at me and asked the ranger, "Can she go with us?" My heart melted.

I made a deal with the ranger: If he would guard our cabin, the kids could sleep on our couch until their grandparents arrived. As they left the cabin, they paused to thank the strangers who had opened their doors.

Take a look at their faces, I told the children, trying to channel Mister Rogers. There are helpers everywhere. Don't ever forget that. There is always help and there is always hope.

You found hope at Lake Hope, I told them. We all laughed.

"We're not tired," the two children sang in unison as we tucked pillows under their heads and turned the lights low. They were sound asleep in seconds. I sat in a nearby chair to make sure they were safe.

At 1:30 a.m. a car pulled up. Their grandparents had come to retrieve them. My daughter and her husband talked to them outside about getting help for the kids and their mom, to help her quit drinking.

I felt the deepest peace inside. What an honor to have met these children, these two beautiful souls who had felt so hopeless but helped all of us see that hope is all around us.

I paused and prayed over them and asked God to protect them. Then I wrote each child a tiny note telling them how brave they were, and that we would be with them in spirit. I tucked it in their backpack. My daughter tucked in the Uno game.

Her husband carried each sleeping child to their car. That's when I realized it was Father's Day. It was Sunday. He was doing his fatherly duty for these children.

We waved as they drove away into the dark.

Those two little ones just might be the bravest people I have ever met.

In the middle of nowhere, in their darkest night when they felt they had lost all hope, they kept looking and found it.

Or maybe it found us all.

12

Mind your own soul.

My older sister Mary woke up my soul.

She sent me an email giving me an update on what was going on in her life, then wrote at the end, "I am living the life my soul wants to have."

Wow. Am I?

Are you?

I never looked at it that way. What would that kind of life look like? Can I really simply live the life my soul wants me to live?

How do you know what that is? Your soul knows. It's not the resume life so many of us pursue. It's what Arianna Huffington calls "the eulogy life."

Rumi once wrote, "The soul is here for its own joy." What is the soul? The highest Self, the God within, the Holy Spirit, the spirit of Truth that abides within us all.

What I do know for sure is I spend too much physical, emotional, and spiritual energy trying to mind everyone else's life, as if my gossip and critiques and judgment will make a difference. My friend Katie often reminds me, "Not my circus; not my monkeys."

Other peoples' lives and decisions fall in the category of None of My Business. I agree with Kris Carr, the inspirational cancer survivor and author who said, "The only time you can change someone is when they are in diapers."

When you're minding other people's energy, you're wasting your own.

One of my spiritual advisors, Lynn McCown, recommended I ask my soul this question before I get out of bed every morning: "Soul, is there anything I need to know today?"

Then I pause and listen. The answer always comes gently as a feather landing on my pillow.

Be in the moment. Be still. Be good to you today. Be present in today. Be gentle with yourself. Be here. Be happy. Love yourself as is. All is well. Go easy on yourself today. Just love your life. Do what comes easy. Take really good care of yourself today. Sleep. Rest. Relax. The key is alignment. Save some of this day for you. Just love your life. Just do the next right thing. Ground. Pour love all over today. Float. Mind your own soul. Love and honor you. Go love your life.

The words are always a mantra of kindness and calm. They are never mean or harsh.

After I ask the question and write down the answer, I ask for the grace to live the life my soul wants me to live, then I give thanks for that grace and go about my day.

Some mornings, I strike a metal singing bowl with the wooden mallet and stand above it so the vibrations flow through me. The energy from the waves of sound seems to comfort and align any scattered energy in me.

My soul used to feel so scattered. A few spiritual advisors and counselors told me child abuse can shatter a child's soul, and the pieces stay scattered until the adult self gathers them up. One year when I headed out to Phoenix, I read a book on soul retrieval on the plane and thought about all the broken pieces of my life that felt like soul losses, the abuse, neglect, and betrayals.

My sister Joan and I drove to Sedona that trip and sat to meditate in what they say is a "spiritual energy vortex." I leaned against one mountain and faced another and let my body rest. After an hour, I felt moved to sit in the vortex in the middle. There I gathered nearby stones and build a cairn, a stack of smooth, flat rocks. I made the altar at the feet of a crooked, twisty, juniper tree.

I set down the first big rock to honor me as I was before birth, a blueprint in the cosmos, a thought of God, a handful of stardust.

Then I whispered a prayer, "Heal me at 1, at 2, at 3... and so on up to age 6 when I was sexually abused." I added another rock and swirled my fingers around the surface and prayed for healing the child I was at 6, 7, 8, 9 and 10. Then I added another rock for when I gave up on love at those railroad tracks.

"Heal me at 10, 11, 12," I prayed, and so on up to 17, when I was raped by a high school football player.

Then I added another rock to heal me at 18, 19, 20, and 21, when I was raped by a college athlete. Then another rock to heal me at every other turn and twist on the broken road and all those bumpy relationships and the cancer journey—all the way up to who I am today.

The words of one psalm I've prayed so often during times of desperation came to me: "You are my strength and my song, my rock, my salvation. I shall not be moved."

Before leaving Sedona, I walked a labyrinth at midnight. The

Lodge at Sedona has a seven-path classical labyrinth that is both a geometric form and spiritual path.

It looks like a maze, but most mazes have a different beginning and ending. Not a labyrinth; there aren't any choices to make except one: Will you enter? Its only path leads to the center, then back out again. It winds, and just when you think you're near the center, it turns left or right.

Before entering, I got quiet and felt my feet on the earth. I heard the words "I Am" whispered, no, more like *breathed* into me. The stars in the Sedona sky twinkled and blinked and winked at me.

I walked the labyrinth again in the cool morning before sunrise. I set out to go barefoot but the rocks hurt. No more suffering; that is not my path, so I put my sandals back on.

As I walked, the words "I Am" helped me surrender all the identities at every turn: writer, author, columnist, journalist, mother, wife, daughter, sister, aunt, neighbor, speaker, grandmother, stepmother, woman. I surrendered them all for a blank slate, "I AM."

My soul gave me a blank slate.

I smiled as I felt myself call my soul back home, "All ee, all ee, in free." After all these years, our game of hide and seek was over. Soul, come back. It's safe to return. I will protect you. I will embrace you. I will love you.

Or maybe it was my soul calling me back home. It didn't matter which. I was ready to welcome all of me back, every age, every fragmented piece.

I was finally ready to live the life my soul wants me to live.

13

Life is a gift. Pass it on.

The gift of life can take your breath away.

Lynda Corea will never forget the simple sound of her son's lungs breathing in and out.

Mike was born with a rare liver disease in 1983. He had surgery when he was five weeks old, but the doctors at Rainbow Babies & Children's Hospital in Cleveland said he wouldn't live long. Maybe six months. They knew his liver wouldn't last long.

The Coreas took him home and loved him. Mike sat. He crawled. He walked. The doctors gave him two years. Mike made it to 11 years old but grew sick fast. He had no energy. His skin turned yellow. He had diarrhea every day.

For two years he waited on a transplant list. His parents wore a pager every day. They couldn't travel more than 50 miles from the hospital. Mike never talked about high school. He never talked about having a future.

At 13, he ended up in the hospital for three weeks. They prepared for him to die. Mike wrote out his will—twice. His parents weren't sure what was next when they took him home. That same day, they got the call.

A 17-year-old girl from Toledo had died in a car accident. When he learned the liver might be a match, Mike went into his room and sat in his closet for two hours. He had to make peace with receiving her liver and make peace with having a surgery that he might not survive.

When he came out, he told his parents he was no longer afraid to die.

"If I die, you let them take anything they want so others can live," he told his mom.

Mike got the girl's liver that February of 1997. It allowed him to go to high school, to run track, to play baseball. He was a wiz at math and graduated from high school with honors. He went to the only school he applied to, The Ohio State University. He majored in finance and planned to go to law school. He finished his last final that June of 2006.

He called his mom after his last exam. He was ready to celebrate. He told her he planned to relax, lift weights, then ride his motorcycle. She couldn't wait to see him later that week at graduation. They talked for 20 minutes. He told his mom he was on top of the world and free. She told him she loved him.

It was their last conversation.

Lynda got the call at midnight.

"Your son was in an accident. You need to come down to the Ohio State University Medical Center," a voice on the phone said.

Mike had been riding his blue and white Suzuki 650 motorcycle. The driver of the car didn't see him. Mike flew 30 feet in the air and landed on his head. Even with a helmet, his injuries were severe.

Mike's family rushed to the Ohio State University Medical

Center in Columbus. Mike was in a coma on a ventilator. The doctors couldn't stop the bleeding and swelling in his brain. Lynda knew he was dying.

So did her daughter, Jessica. She asked the hospital staff to call Ohio State and have them bring Mike's diploma to the hospital. Graduation day was just six days away. Mike wouldn't live to walk across the stage, but they wanted him to graduate before he died.

Two hours later, someone showed up at the hospital with his diploma. His sister read the words out loud to him. Mike died a graduate of Ohio State University. He was 22.

He donated his heart, lungs, corneas, skin, tendons, ligaments, and long bones.

At his funeral, Lynda felt peace knowing they had fulfilled his wishes and given life to others, that she was able to pass on her son's life. She also knew Mike died doing what he loved, riding his motorcycle. He once said, "When I die, I hope I die on my bike, because I'll die happy."

Lynda still prays for the woman who hit him. That woman graduated the same day Mike would have. Her name was near his name on the graduation program.

Lynda wanted to connect with the people who got her son's organs. After Mike got a liver, Lynda had written the parents whose daughter had donated it. The girl's mom wrote for a while, but it was too painful for her to continue, and they never met.

Requests to connect with a recipient go through the organ procurement team. The process is to have the letters exchanged anonymously, then, in time, if both parties want to, they can decide how and where to meet. The woman who got Mike's lungs wrote back. She was the mother of four and the grand-mother of twelve.

Those letters would bring about healing for both women.

The women decided to meet two years after exchanging letters. Barb lived south of Pittsburgh, and Lynda lived in Ohio about two hours away. They met at a restaurant halfway. They talked for a while, then went to the restroom. Barb looked at Lynda and her daughter and paused.

"Put your head on my chest and feel Mike's lungs," she said.

Lynda and Jessica rested their heads against Barb's chest and listened. Every breath Barb took came from Mike's lungs. They all cried. Lynda could have stayed there forever listening to those precious breaths.

Finally, Lynda took in a breath and said, "They aren't Mike's lungs anymore. They're yours."

"I will take the best care of them," Barb said.

She did until she died in 2022. Her lungs were still good, but her kidneys were damaged by the anti-rejection medicine. Barb had spent every day grateful for Mike's gift of life.

Lynda went to her funeral and was overwhelmed by the trib-ute to Mike and his gift of life to Barb. Her grandchildren and great grandchildren told Lynda, if it wasn't for Mike's gift, they would have never known their grandmother. They thanked her profusely.

Lynda is grateful she got Mike for 22 years. "I have many more smiles than I have tears," she said. "I truly believe Mike's work was done, but mine wasn't."

When I met her, Lynda was a volunteer at Lifebanc, a non-profit organ procurement agency that serves most of Northeast Ohio. The more people like Lynda spread the message, the more donors sign up to save lives.

Her son was grateful every day of his life for the new life someone else gave him, and so was Lynda. Every day, 16 people in the United States die because the life-giving organ they need isn't available. There are 103,000 on the waiting list for organs.

Lynda knows the joy of receiving life and the bittersweet joy of giving it. Mike is one of a handful of people in the country who has been both an organ recipient and an organ donor.

To register as an organ, eye, and tissue donor, you can contact the Bureau of Motor Vehicles. Or you can register online at www.lifebanc.org or call Lifebanc at 888-558-LIFE (5433) for a registration form.

One organ donor has the power to save and heal eight lives. One organ, eye, and tissue donor can impact more than 50 lives.

Life is a gift.

Pass it on.

14

If you believe you can handle anything, you can.

You can handle it.

All of it.

No matter what it is.

I use it as a mantra: "I can handle this."

My friend Ro Eugene used to say, "Life is hard, but you can do hard. It's not impossible; it's just life."

Everyone has a different version of hard. And the hard keeps changing because life is a moving target. Nothing stays still for long. Stuff shows up at random. We call them problems, difficulties, and disappointments, but it's all just life.

It's the part of life we think we don't want, yet in that rearview mirror, it often becomes the best part.

I've learned that from my own life and from working with Glenn Proctor, a tough journalist who always had your back. The Marine Corps trained him well. So did life. It kept knocking him down, and he kept getting back up. The U.S. Marine Corps trained him to find the strength inside that is always there and to rely on it no matter what life throws your way.

Glenn has packed more lives into one than most people. We

were both business writers at the *Beacon Journal* in Akron, Ohio. He helped the newspaper win a Pulitzer Prize covering the 1986 hostile takeover attempt of the Goodyear Tire and Rubber Co., Akron's biggest employer back then.

He was the tender, tough guy who challenged you to do your best and always had your back if anyone gave you grief.

I didn't know his entire back story until years after we worked together. He ended up a foster child at age 3, living mostly with his grandparents and on and off with other relatives in the Philadelphia area. His aunt was like a drill instructor, a mix of tender and tough. Even with his grandparents, who were older and sometimes sick, he got shuffled around, living on and off with other relatives.

At 8 years old, he wrote poems about being in foster care that helped him cope. Poetry was his lifeline before and after he started drinking beer and wine at 12, then hard liquor at 13.

As a teen, he was told to work in the mill or join the military, so he joined the U.S. Marine Corps, the toughest branch of the U.S. military. He knew they would make him or break him. Boot camp was the shock of his life. Back when he joined, if you were the last recruit off the bus, the drill sergeant slugged you in the jaw.

He served six years on active duty, including 13 months in the Vietnam War.

"I still love the uniform. I learned the blood stripe (worn by enlisted noncommissioned officers and officers) represented all the Marines that passed and came before you," he said. "I loved every button in place and shoeshine, how squared away they were. I wanted to be one of them."

The greatest lesson they taught?

"The absolute belief that I can do whatever needs done," he said. "I call on that every day, especially when I talk to folks about suicide and how tough it can be."

His grandmother was his main caretaker, his grandfather the enforcer. His Aunt Elsie was the drill instructor. He lost his grandfather to suicide.

"I was in the next room when he took his life," he said. "I heard the shot." Glenn was 23 when it happened.

"The why stays with you forever. The why never goes away," he said. "You try to compartmentalize it, but it always stays there. You continue to grieve. It goes and comes."

He took suicide prevention courses and works with veterans and parents who lost children to suicide. He worked with one mother whose child attempted suicide twice at six years old. Six.

He's also a recovering alcoholic.

"I was a big-time bottle drunk," he said. "I was angry for a lot of years. Deep down on the other side of me, I knew I could deal with anything." He spent 30 days in rehab in 1984. He quit drinking when a fellow Marine and Vietnam vet told him he was going to die in a ditch if he didn't quit.

Journalism called to him one day when a shooting happened in the small town where his grandparents lived in Pennsylvania. He watched reporters cover it and thought, "I can do that," and got the name of one reporter. He called to talk to him about writing. Glenn had no writing samples, just poetry. Yellowed, old poems. But his writing impressed the editors, so they hired him. He had no college degree but enough talent to launch a four-decade career in journalism.

The walk-on reporter with no high school or college journalism training later became vice president/news and executive editor of the *Richmond Times-Dispatch,* a Pulitzer Prize winner, a five-time Pulitzer Prize judge, and a journalism/media management professor and mentor to hundreds of journalists, career professionals, veterans, and students over a 40-year career, spanning from 1970 to 2011.

Now he operates writing boot camps for adults, many of whom are working on their first books. A dozen have become published authors.

After he retired from journalism, he founded his own coaching business. He became a suicide prevention instructor and grief support counselor. He gets into the hardest part of people's lives. He lives in Charlotte, North Carolina, where he offers life coaching, mental health first aid, and suicide prevention guidance.

He's been married and divorced and was a single parent with custody of two kids. He also survived prostate cancer.

He runs on grit, grace, gratitude, and faith in a God he calls, "The Good Brother." Glenn, a former Marine Corps gunnery sergeant, is also the author of five books, including a poetry trilogy. He teaches and trains from his life experience, sharing all the lessons he learned as a foster child, single parent, alcoholic, Marine, Vietnam vet, and cancer survivor.

Glenn has a lifetime of lessons to guide others:

The thing to remember about the curves, turns, stops, and starts of life is that you're doing the driving.

Accept your life story or remain in first gear. It's up to you to shift gears on your life.

Carry your own water. Teams are essential, but you have to carry your own weight.

Believe and love the face in the mirror. Be true to yourself or you can't be true to others.

Never say "I wish." Say "I did." Die with no regrets.

If you think the mountain is too high, then it is. Don't be upset when others climb over you.

Everyone has made and will make mistakes. How we bounce back is what counts. When you fall, don't get up, jump up.

Glenn had a hard life, but he uses that hard life to make life easier for others.

He tells them what he told himself all along:

This is hard, but you can do hard.

15

*Be prepared for anything
so you can enjoy everything.*

There were a lot of reasons *not* to go on a five-day backpacking trip in Wild and Wonderful West Virginia, but I didn't want any single one of them to stop me.

For decades, I had wanted to go back to the hills of West Virginia that I hiked back when I was 20 and a college student with nothing to fear. But that had been 42 years ago.

Was it too late? Was I too old? Was there any wild left in me?

There aren't many truly wild places left that haven't been tamed. Dolly Sods Wilderness is just a five-and-a-half-hour drive away, almost three hundred miles from my home in Cleveland.

Dolly Sods is an official U.S. Wilderness Area in the Allegheny Mountains of eastern West Virginia. It's part of the Monongahela National Forest of the U.S. Forest Service. It consists of creeks and waterfalls, sandstone and red spruce, bogs and meadows, and 17,776 acres with 47 miles of trails over elevations ranging from 2,500 to 4,700 feet.

To guard its pristine, primal nature, they limit groups to ten or fewer.

Way back in college, I trusted my friends to pack what we needed, and I borrowed a backpack from a guy I was dating. We ate freeze-dried food we boiled in water over a fire. We slid down waterfalls in the sun. Then a snowstorm hit during the night. We huddled together in the tent for warmth. In the morning, the creek we had easily crossed the day before had become a raging river.

We lugged a big tree trunk over the shallowest part to cross. One woman fell in. She couldn't get out. Her backpack weighed her down, so another person jumped in to save her. They were walking icicles by the time we got back to the car five miles away.

The best part? Climbing straight up to reach Lion's Head on Breathed Mountain. We hiked uphill for three miles, the last stretch, over giant boulders. Standing on top, we saw God's view of the world. No power lines. No houses. Just endless mountaintops and wilderness. It's why they call West Virginia "Almost Heaven."

My daughter did the same backpacking trip when she was in college. I wanted to take this trip with her, but her three young children needed her, so she couldn't join me. I didn't want to die without going again, so I went with a group of nine total strangers. The Cleveland Metroparks organized the five-day trip with two guides.

Was I too old for a backcountry adventure of five days in the wilderness at age 62? Too old? No way. It was time to be bold. Go bold or go home.

Grandma Gatewood inspired me. She survived a tough life of domestic violence, living on a farm raising 11 children. One day she told her grown kids she was going for a walk. She left and hiked the Appalachian Trail. All 2,168 miles (3,489 km) of it.

At the time, Emma Rowena Gatewood was 67. She was the first ever solo woman to walk the entire length. That was back in 1955, before you could buy everything you needed on the internet.

She invented ultralight. She packed a shower curtain, wore sneakers, carried a few clothes and food in a homemade bag that she slung over her shoulder. Some nights, she slept on leaves or heated flat stones near a campfire to use as a warm bed.

She also was the first person ever to hike the Appalachian Trail three times. I read her book to convince me I wasn't too old. The first time she tried, she got lost, broke her glasses, and ran out of food. She went back and did it better.

To prepare, for a few weeks I hiked every day with weights in my backpack to get strong. I would have to carry everything—food, water, clothes, tent, sleeping bag, first aid kit. This was wilderness, so there would be no picnic tables, few trail markers, and no restrooms.

You had to carry your own small shovel, dig a hole, do your business, and leave no trace, which meant carrying out used toilet paper. Gross but true, so the bears wouldn't dig it up.

First, I made a list of everything I hated about camping, which was a lot. I wrote down every potential problem so I could then find a solution to match. I also jotted down all my fears, starting with the biggest one: Bears.

There would be black bears, so you can't leave any food out. You must tie it up in a sack at night and keep it elevated between trees. Or put it in a Bear Vault, a big, hard, plastic canister that bears can't open.

I imagined putting all my fears in that container and called it the "Fear Vault." I feared getting attacked by a bear, bit by a rattlesnake, or getting lost.

What if I can't carry 25 to 35 pounds on my back all day? What if I'm cold all night? Or too scared to sleep? What if I'm too slow for the group? What if I get homesick for the grand-kids, my hubby, my bed, and my bathroom?

Ah, but this deep, green earth *is* my home, I reminded myself. And the God who loves me was going with me.

I had to keep sight of my why. Remember your "why." Mine? I wanted to connect with the me who once loved the Earth fiercely and fearlessly. I was forgetting who I was. I needed to connect to the Universe, to participate fully in life, to scream my holy "YES!" to life.

This would be a retreat of sorts. The Earth was my retreat house, my cathedral, my chapel, my holy ground, my rock, and my shelter.

Henry David Thoreau gave me my "why" way back when I first discovered *Walden* in high school with these words:

"I went into the woods because I wished to live deliberately, to front only the essential facts of life, and see if I could not learn what it had to teach, and not, when I came to die, discover that I had not lived. I did not wish to live what was not life, living is so dear."

I didn't do it as simply as he did, though. I carried a solution for every problem I was likely to encounter:

I didn't want to get Lyme disease from a tick, so I packed tweezers, a tick remover, and a small mirror for those hard-to-see private places: under my knees, armpits, and ankles. I covered my hiking shoes, pants, backpack, and tent with bug spray.

Bears? At least they would be black bears, not grizzly bears.

Still, a bear can smell your lip balm three miles away. Do we bring bear spray? Wear bells so they hear us? We would be vigilant hanging up all the food at night and never eat in our tents.

I also knew to bring no cotton clothes. You wear wool or fleece that dries fast.

To start a fire, I packed cotton balls dipped in Vaseline in a tiny plastic bag and brought waterproof matches.

For the cold, I bought the warmest sleeping bag I could find and packed an emergency foil blanket, thin down jacket, gloves, and hand warmers to tuck into my sleeping bag 30 minutes before tucking me in it.

I also brought rain pants, a warm hat, gloves, and waterproof boots.

To keep from getting lost, I brought a compass and maps.

For muscle aches, I packed blister bandages, Tylenol, and new sock liners.

For food, I packed the same lunch every day: peanut butter, bread, carrots, and cheese with crackers.

"Overprepare and go with the flow" was my motto. And speaking of flow, the one thing I wanted to avoid most was getting up to pee three times a night in the dark. I didn't want to be surprised by a skunk, a snake, or poison ivy while squatting to answer Mother Nature's call. Plus, it's hard to squat to pee with 30 pounds on your back while you're hiking. When nature calls and you're 62, she has you on speed dial.

I researched "feminine urinary devices" and bought a pee funnel. Ladies, the struggle is real. I discovered so many options: The Tinkle Bell, the Pibella, which sounded Italian, like a red wine: "I'll have a little Pibella with my pasta." The SheWee, the Go Girl "don't take life sitting down," Lady P., Whiz Freedom, and PStyle, which resembles a tiny water slide. I bought that one and practiced in the shower.

On the trail, you just unzip your jeans, scoot your undies to the side, tuck the funnel against your skin for a tight seal, point it down, relax, and wee! Gravity does the rest. Done? Shake it like a guy and wipe the funnel clean with a pee rag. Yes, there is such a thing. It's a bandanna with one sole purpose.

I loved the pee funnel so much I might just use it in winter to write my name in the snow like guys do.

The first night I set up my tent, a dozen notes fell out. My grandkids and their parents had tucked inspiration in everywhere. One note read, "You are fleece." Oh wait, I misread it. It said, "You are fierce!"

Five days in the wilderness taught me to be wild, along with a host of other lessons:

Embrace the suck. And some moments *will* suck.

Don't feed your fears and they won't grow.

Water is life. Always refill it and keep it clean.

Hike your own hike. Don't compare yourself to anyone else.

No one ever made a fire with clean hands. Don't be afraid of dirt.

Anything you want to bring must be worth the weight it adds to your back.

Don't quit on a bad day, no matter how tempted you are.

Everything hard eventually ends. Hang in there.

Put your rain pants on *before* it starts to rain.

Pack the solution for every potential problem.

What you focus on grows.

Gather wood *before* it rains.

A bent leaf can turn into a water spigot to fill your bottle in a stream.

Listen to everything. The pine needles, the rain, the river, even the stars have a message for you.

Appreciate the small stuff: a breeze, chili in a baggie, a spork, clean undies, and dry socks.

The third night we camped near a waterfall. It rained all night. It was noisy, but not a drop touched me. I wrapped myself up like a human burrito inside my tent.

The roughest part? Tripping over roots, stumbling over rocks, encountering false trails, dead ends, twists and turns that went nowhere, and stepping in gooey pile of poo a fellow hiker didn't bother to bury.

I kept telling myself, it's all worth it for that view.

Then the guide announced we might have to skip Lion's Head, the most amazing part of the trip. One hiker hadn't prepared well for the trip. She didn't break in her new shoes and got blisters. It might be too hard for her to walk.

My heart was crushed.

I hadn't seen Lion's Head in 42 years. We came this far and we're going to skip it because of her blisters? NO! This was my dream trip, and that was the pinnacle. How could we skip the very best part of Dolly Sods?

"Nooo!" my heart cried, but I would have to let the Universe decide. So I surrendered to life. I shared what I had prepared for me and gave the woman my brand-new sock liners to comfort her blisters.

The guides were able to bandage her feet up, and we continued. We hiked the long, rocky path through rhododendron tunnels and climbed giant boulders to reach the top.

There, there it was. More breathtaking than I remember.

That spot where I stood at 20. Where my daughter stood at 20.

It felt so holy, I took off my shoes and socks. I slowly turned around and around to see mountains, mountains, and more mountains.

Then I lay down for as long as I could on that massive rock of Earth, my Home, my slice of Heaven. I felt fleece . . . I mean fierce.

16

Don't lose your wild.

Too many adults live restrained, careful, boring lives. Most children don't. They haven't lost their spark. Don't lose yours.

One Mother's Day, my eight-year-old granddaughter thought it would be fun to roll down a hill at her sister's soccer game. She was bored just watching other kids play soccer, so she wandered off.

We were busy watching the game while she ran around with another little girl. She didn't know that grassy green slope ended up in a huge puddle. She got covered in mud from her neck to her toes. Her entire right side was a smear of mud. She laughed herself silly, even as she took off her chilly wet clothes in the nearest bathroom and climbed into extra clothes her mom had in the car.

She didn't seem bothered one bit that she was covered in mud. She was pleasantly surprised at the turn of events. She went from a simple roll down a hill to a soaked mess.

I loved her pure joy. No embarrassment. No shame. No regret. Just joy. I went to bed thinking about her glee and wondered, *When was the last time I did something that bold and silly?*

My youngest grandchild was born bold. When she was

seven, she wrote the President of the United States a letter. She wanted him to change the word "history" to "past stories" because "history" has the word "his" in it. As she pointed out in her penciled letter, "But there are girls in history not just men. Please write back."

A year later, he did. President Joe Biden sent her a letter telling her she had the power to "impact the future for your generation and generations to come. I urge you to remain curious, creative and fearless."

I think she will.

She's the kid who collects bugs and saves her used Band-Aids to remember how she earned them. They are badges of honor in her little world. She shows off every scab and sore and cut and bruise. She's the one who runs barefoot in the snow, dances in the rain, and rarely brushes her hair. She'll leave for school with her hair in orderly, beautiful French braids created by her mom, then get off the bus hours later with her hair long and loose, wild and free. She's the one who gets excited over finding animal bones on nature hikes and brings them to school. She's such a free spirit.

I was once one, too. So were you.

The day after she ran down that muddy hill, I whispered to her, "Don't ever lose your wild."

Too many of us do. We become some perfect orderly sanitized version of ourselves. We set out to make a New and Improved version of ourselves every year. We craft endless goals and to-do lists. We lose sight of the original blessing we were designed and called to be.

We're each a beautiful, messy masterpiece, one wild, unique creation with God's fingerprints all over us.

How do you not lose your wild?

Get out in the wild. Take the messy trail, not the paved one. Get dirty—your hands, your feet, your face. Go barefoot on the grass. Pick wildflowers. Roll down the nearest hill.

Wear what you love. If you're 85 and you love that bikini, rock it! I just bought bright aqua sneakers. If you've got a pair of screaming red shoes, wear them. All my sneakers used to be white or black. Not anymore! Go bold or go home.

Howl at the moon. Get out there tonight and search the stars. You are stardust. How wild is that! Dance in the moonlight. Breathe in the night. Chase lightning bugs.

Read wild books. *Eat, Pray, Love*, by Elizabeth Gilbert. *Wild*, by Cheryl Strayed. *Untamed*, by Glennon Doyle. Read poems by Billy Collins, Maya Angelou, and Mary Oliver to decide how to spend this wild and precious day.

Act like a child. Hop on the nearest swing set and try to reach Mars. Eat ice cream for breakfast. Wear clothes that don't match. Put on a tutu and tights. Wear face paint or a stick-on unicorn tattoo. Roll down the car windows no matter how cold it is outside.

Create something wicked and wild. Throw paint across an old bed sheet and hang it up as a tapestry. Chalk the sidewalk. Gather 12 odd objects from nature and make a work of art.

Do something that scares you. If life scares you, scare it back. Yell BOO! first. My granddaughter taught me at 65 how to Rollerblade. First lesson? How to fall. I got an A+. And a few new bruises.

Hang out with wild friends. Can't find anyone to kayak, camp, or hike with? Get some new friends. Create an Adventure Club. Write down all the fun stuff you want to try: Ride horses, rock climb, paddleboard. Then make a list of all the fun people in your life that will do it with you.

Make a playlist to feed your wild soul. Add every song that makes you feel so wild and free that you can't help but dance, or just add songs that fill your soul. When I turned 60, my friend Derdriu collected 60 songs on three CDs for me to take to Ireland to celebrate. She's from Ireland, so she picked out the perfect music for driving around the Emerald Isle.

Get lost. Hop in the car, put away your phone, and start driving. See where the highway takes you. Get on a train and get off at a stop you've never seen. Ride the subway and explore a new side of the city. Take a different way to work.

Love yourself bigger and bolder than ever. Stand naked in front of the mirror and tell every single inch of you how much you love it, *as is*. Go wild over every scar, wrinkle, and birthmark. Listen to its story. That scar on my knee? We crashed in my brother's homemade Soap Box Derby car on the railroad tracks when I was 10. Those scars on my chest? I fought cancer and won. Those scars are badges of honor. So are yours.

Every day, energize. Pound on your chest like a gorilla. Sing at the top of your lungs in your car, in the shower, in the front yard. Do ten jumping jacks. Start your morning listening to Queen singing "Don't Stop Me Now." Crank it up loud, and sing along so you don't hit the brakes on life.

Now, go hit the gas, or the nearest hill, and see where life takes you on this wild, wonderful journey.

17

Getting lost could be the best part of the journey.

Getting lost is a fine art that's fading away.

I blame GPS, apps like Waze, Google Maps, and people like me who depend way too much on them.

My daughter is a human compass. Spin her around blindfolded eight times and she'll still know which direction is north.

Me? I'm the opposite of a compass. My magnetic north points to Lost. I once drove the wrong direction on an interstate across America for two hours. I was heading east to Virginia Beach with a boyfriend, who dozed off while I was driving. When he woke up two hours later, he said the scenery looked too familiar. Turns out when I got back on the interstate after getting gas, I took the ramp heading west, not east.

When I bought my last car, I paid to have a compass installed so the directional letters for North, South, East, and West light up red inside the rearview mirror. It's the only way I know east from west. You can't just look up in the sky in Cleveland to see which direction the sun is shining. The cloud coverage from Lake Erie blots out the sun most days, so you can't really tell where the sun is. I blame the Lake Effect for the clouds (and for everything from bad weather to our beloved Browns losing).

But I read an article that said getting lost could be a blessing. It stimulates the brain by activating the hippocampus, which keeps the brain from shrinking.

In an article in the *Washington Post,* M. R. O'Connor wrote that our brains are changing when we rely too much on gadgets for directions.

"When people are told which way to turn, it relieves them of the need to create their own routes and remember them," O'Connor wrote. "They pay less attention to their surroundings. And neuroscientists can now see that brain behavior changes when people rely on turn-by-turn directions."

She quoted Amir-Homayoun Javadi, the author of a study published in *Nature Communications* in 2017, who discovered, "When people use tools such as GPS, they tend to engage less with navigation. Therefore, brain area responsible for navigation is less used, and consequently their brain areas involved in navigation tend to shrink."

Ever since I went backpacking in West Virginia, I've been trying to expand my brain by practicing orienteering.

"Always know in what direction you are headed," a hiker advised. I test myself daily. And fail way too often.

I do love spreading out a paper map to find my way. I keep an atlas of the United States in my car trunk just in case there's ever an emergency and I need to hit the road and keep moving. When I traveled to Poland for book signings, I carried a printed map of Krakow and Warsaw, just to orient myself to both glorious cities so I wouldn't miss out on any interesting monuments, memorials, or wonders. When I traveled by train across Ireland from Belfast to Cork, I loved following the map to see the names of the rivers and roads we passed.

Everyone has a map on their smartphone, but I still like one you can touch and spread out. A few years ago, two lost college guys were hanging outside a local Starbucks in need of directions to get to a city outside of Pittsburgh, just two hours from where we were standing.

Their phone had died. When I pulled out a paper map to help them, they burst out laughing.

"You still use a map?" they chortled.

They stopped laughing when I reminded them, "I'm not the one who's lost."

Most people depend on GPS to get them where they want to go. But how do you get to places you didn't know you wanted to go? That's the joy of getting lost. You stop and ask directions. You meet people along the way. Strangers become instant friends. You run across a peach stand on a back road or discover an ice cream stand or a local restaurant and eat a meal you'll never forget. You discover parts of your country you didn't plan on visiting.

Once on our annual vacation to the Outer Banks of North Carolina, I took the wrong highway when my husband was asleep. (Yes, there's a pattern here. If you're riding with me, don't fall asleep or you'll wake up in Poughkeepsie or Peoria.) When he woke up, we were on the Lincoln Highway that runs east and west across the United States. A huge mountain stood in front of us.

Turns out his great uncle had hiked the entire Lincoln Highway in 1914, so we enjoyed the detour, even though it took us an hour longer to get home. We got to see a slice of the journey his great uncle took.

What's the hurry?

My kids use traffic apps to speed up every journey. The GPS navigation tools help them shave five minutes off a 15-minute trip and avoid any accidents or traffic. Their favorite app is updated by drivers to show the fastest way to wherever you're going and how to bypass construction or traffic accidents. But isn't life supposed to be about enjoying the journey, not just rushing to the destination?

I still remember following signs for a detour on my way home from the University of Notre Dame in Indiana after watching my niece in the marching band. I carefully followed all those signs but somehow wound up in a cornfield. I laughed myself silly. I ended up on back roads and gravel roads and felt wild and free. The smaller the towns got, the more fun I had stopping for ice cream and fresh tomatoes along the roadside.

J. R. R. Tolkien once wrote, "Not all those who wander are lost."

Sometimes I get lost on purpose—just take a random left or right and let the road lead me, just to follow it and see where it leads. There's a joy in letting the world reveal itself to you, to take the lead in this great dance of life.

Instead of leading the dance, follow. The journey itself might be a wild adventure.

Get lost.

Put *that* on your bucket list.

18

*The only limits you have are
the ones you give yourself.*

Nothing stops Jon Sedor.

Nothing.

When he lost his dominant left hand to an accident at 18 years old, he trained his other hand to write, type, and draw. And make art. And surf. And rock climb.

Yes, rock climb. We're talking the Grand Teton, the highest peak in Wyoming, at 13,775 feet high.

Nothing stops Jon. Not even a diagnosis of brain cancer. When he was told he might have just two years to live, he got busy living—deeper, louder, and bolder.

In spite of radiation and chemo treatments, he's been busy creating murals to inspire and challenge people to do more and to be more.

Jon is an artist who specializes in graphic design and street art. He was born in Cleveland, Ohio, in May 1988. He became fascinated with art in the world of skateboarding, BMX, and graffiti culture when he was 13.

In high school, he decided to pursue it as a career. A week before Jon graduated, in May 2007, he and some friends were goofing off with fireworks and a demolition device. It exploded in his hand.

"I heard a pop, then saw things flying," he said.

The accident destroyed his hand. He underwent three surgeries and two amputations. He ultimately lost his hand.

"It was just an accident," he said. "Ninety-nine percent of people get away with those things. I was the one percent."

His life changed in a flash.

"The important thing I took away from it is how fast everything can change," he said.

He entered college as an art major just 12 weeks after losing his hand. But he could no longer ride BMX.

"I had to figure out my life all over again," he said. "I stuck with the art part, but it took a while to find myself again."

He didn't give up on his dreams. He just recreated them. Now he creates and lives as a right-handed person. Jon had to train his right hand to become his dominant hand.

"In time, my brain adapted," he said. "I didn't really have a choice. When you lose your dominant hand, you can't slowly ease into changing. You just have to do it. It made me grow up in a lot of ways."

Art has always been his outlet. "It sort of saved my life. I was getting into trouble my freshman year and had a very bad grade point average; I just didn't like school."

A teacher sat him down and asked, *What do you like to do outside of school?*

"I like graffiti and I like BMX," Jon told him.

So the teacher got him into an art class, and they let him ride BMX and his skateboard as credit for his gym class. His high school advisor and art teacher visited him in the hospital. They encouraged him and challenged him. Jon had to relearn how to write and draw.

After he lost his hand, he graduated from Skidmore College in New York as a studio art major. He studied at the School of the Art Institute of Chicago, then graduated from the School of Visual Arts in Manhattan with a master's in fine arts.

His art took off. He created a 12- by 25-foot indoor mural at the Music Settlement community music school's new campus in Ohio City and several outdoor murals in Ohio: one on the banks of Lake Erie, one in Shaker Heights, and a 24- by 23-foot wall in Tennessee, at a business run by a friend who happens to be a leg amputee Jon met while competing in para-climbing events.

Four years after the accident, he quit smoking to get his lungs stronger to go rock climbing. He uses his left arm to push off rocks. He uses his arms as independent tools. He uses the stump of his left arm for pushing and balance, to keep his body into the wall while his right hand reaches for the next rock.

"There's still a lot of things I can't climb," he said. "I work in a rock gym. Before, I'd kill myself trying to do everything. I didn't want to be limited. You just have to accept your situation. You gotta know when to push and when to back off."

At his lowest, he just kept looking forward, not back.

"I tried for three or four years to ride BMX. It just wasn't happening." He kept breaking prosthetics.

One day when he was working at a local rock gym feeling disillusioned, someone suggested he teach art. Jon started teaching street art at an inner-city high school for two years at Cleveland School of the Arts.

"Those kids felt like they were my own kids," he said.

He then moved to Florida in 2019. He worked at a behavioral elementary school unit with children. Some kids were in foster care; some didn't speak English. Then he started having migraines.

One night, he had a seizure. His girlfriend called an ambulance. A brain scan at the hospital revealed a tumor the size of a softball in his right frontal lobe.

"I had no idea," he said. "That's the weird thing. I never felt sick, except by the migraines."

He was diagnosed with stage IV glioblastoma brain cancer. He was just 31. He went home to be treated at the Cleveland Clinic.

Surgery removed most of it, but this cancer has no clear borders. Tentacles can spread through his brain. He underwent six weeks of radiation, five days a week, every day, then several rounds of chemo. He lost 40 pounds, and he's a small guy to start with.

He wears a device on his shaved head that looks like a swim cap. It sends low-intensity alternating electric currents, called tumor-treating fields, into Jon's brain cells to stop the cancer from spreading. He has to wear it at least 18 hours a day.

Cancer is a roller coaster of ups and downs, of feeling sick then normal. He tries to balance treatments with living an active life. The prognosis for glioblastoma isn't good, but he's already lived with it since 2019.

Some days he doesn't think about it at all. He rides his bike and surfs with friends. Activity helps center him. If the tumors start growing back, he doesn't know what the next step is, except this: Keep painting. Keep looking forward, not backward.

"It's important for me that I draw every day," he said.

Important to him and to all those who see it.

During the pandemic, he painted a mural to remind people to stick together. He used the side of a building in Shaker Heights as his canvas and painted life-sized muscled arms. The mural was interactive. It invited people to approach it and pose in front of the arms so it looked like the painted muscled arms were theirs. Next to it were the words: "Together we are stronger."

Jon was influenced by tattoo culture and the strong man posters of old. He created his own funky lettering, a knockoff of a tattoo font, and drew blue skin so people of all races could approach it and connect with it. It took him five days to paint because he had to do it between snowfalls so the paint wouldn't freeze. He couldn't use spray paint; it was too windy.

"I wouldn't be where I'm at if I didn't have a group of people that believed in me when I didn't," he said.

During the pandemic and his recovery, community mattered even more. Jon lives and works in Cleveland. He has taught me so much about how to live a life without limits.

"The best thing I do every day is force myself to be creative," Jon said. "That keeps me excited about life."

And everything he creates keeps all those who see it excited about life, a life without limits.

19

No matter what life chooses to give you, choose to receive joy.

The first thing you notice when Katie walks into a room is her smile. She leads with joy. She's like a human sparkler, and the sparks are usually flying all over the place because Katie can't contain all that joy.

She'll tell you an inspirational story or share a quote or some encounter that melted her heart. Or she'll shove a new coffee mug in your face to show you the exciting quote on the side and probably give it to you.

My friend Katie O'Toole Smith packs so much life and joy into every single day. It didn't start out that way. Her dad was an alcoholic. She started drinking at age 11.

"I never thought twice about it," she said. "I just picked it up. I always felt so broken. I was this puzzle piece, and everyone else had their fit around them and I didn't. My brain thought differently. I thought everybody had some kind of manual and knew what the next right thing to do was. When I started drinking, it felt like alcohol filled in those cracks inside of me and made me whole."

She got sober at 16, when most people are just getting started drinking.

Her dad's drinking hurt her, but his sobriety healed her.

"He was the person that I said, 'I never want to be like him,' and I became just like him. Our brains were exactly the same even though our drinking was so different," she said. "When my dad got sober, I watched him change the footprint he left on this Earth through recovery. He got sober in 1984; I got sober in 1987. He connected me into that community. He had a group of people that loved me so much."

What made her quit at 16?

"By the time I entered treatment, I was either going to commit suicide or go down a real bad path," she said. Thank goodness, a social worker in high school intervened.

When people question whether she drank long enough to be an alcoholic, Katie tells them, "Ask my mom if five years was a long time."

It wasn't an easy life. Katie got pregnant and had a baby at 21 and became a single parent. It was back when there was so much shame about having a baby out of wedlock.

"I was terrified. I was in an interracial relationship that wasn't thought of highly in the Irish Catholic community back then," she said. But once her little girl was born, her parents fell in love with their granddaughter.

"My father held her, and I watched him change in front of my eyes," Katie said. Her mom came around and helped her raise her daughter. In time, she married and had two more daughters.

After years of financial struggle, a man at a car-leasing company offered Katie a job answering phones. Katie ended up in a male-dominated industry, selling and leasing cars. People now call her "Katie the Car Lady." She now has her own independent car company whose motto is "Your empowerment is our goal." Katie takes the pressure, stress, and confusion out of buying or leasing a car. She also makes it her mission to educate consumers with tips on how to buy or lease.

Katie is like a matchmaker when it comes to cars. I wanted durability, a car that gets me from Point A to Point B. She put me in a flaming red Subaru Forester that can go off-road when needed.

My husband wanted luxury, so she put him in a Lexus. Katie got our daughter, Gabrielle, in an SUV van big enough for her family of five and Gabrielle's husband in a bright metallic teal Jeep.

Katie pours joy and love into everyone who walks in her door.

"Every single person stands alone. It's about listening to them," she said. "I really believe to put the person first and listen to them. It's never really about the car. It's about the person. I believe if I do the right thing, my business will grow. I love helping people connect dots."

And every day, she chooses joy. It's a joy that comes from living life on life's terms, not from getting her way. What does it mean to choose joy?

You commit to joy daily, no matter what.

No matter what the weather. No matter what the other drivers are doing in front of you. No matter what your spouse or mom or ex did or said to you.

You serve with joy, whether it's making a sandwich for your

child's lunch, serving a stranger food at a restaurant, or sweeping up after someone else's mess.

You smile all day long, not because everything is going your way, but because you have no particular way that it all has to be. Every way is the way of joy.

You give joy away to others so you go to bed empty and let God fill you back up. Katie gives away her joy to her customers, her kids, her spouse, and to women in recovery from alcohol and drug addiction.

In every detour life sent her on, she found women there to help her. She finds joy in helping broken women heal. She tells them not to fear their brokenness.

"Those cracks inside of us are the way God's light gets in," she said. "We see the light in others because that light is already in us. We recognize it."

The key is to be of service where you joyfully want to do it.

Her dad taught her that. After he got sober, he became her hero and role model. He would tell her, "God kissed me on the forehead and gave me another day."

"My dad, God rest his soul, would say, 'God knows where you live, and God knows where you are.'"

Katie gives away a lot of joy. How does she get filled back up?

Her dad used to tell her, we all have a cup inside of us. That cup has to be full. We give away the overflow. If we don't keep it full, we're depleting ourselves.

She fills her joy cup back up every morning.

"My eyes open and before my feet touch the ground, I say, 'Good morning. I choose joy.' No matter what is going on. I choose joy."

Then she has coffee and takes some quiet time. When she looks out the window she says, "Hi, Mother Nature, I see you!" She acknowledges the beauty all around her, even though she lives in northeast Ohio, where Mother Nature isn't always a gentle mother.

Katie sees weather as an adventure and a way to work out her joy muscle. What about when it rains? Free water from the sky! What about when it snows? Make a snow angel!

Surrounding herself with a posse of positive women helps.

"Everyone needs to have a posse. Because it's not about *if* something happens, it's *when* something happens," she said. "Those are the people I check in with. We fill each other up. That's the magic. Someone gives it to you and you give it to someone else and they share it and they share it."

At the end of the day, when she falls into bed, she thanks her Higher Power and the Universe for another day.

She now has a God who loves her.

"I grew up with a punishing God," she said. "I connect to God of joy and love."

She puts that God in the driver's seat every day.

"There are no big deals. Life is short," she said. "Pause. That's where God is. In this moment. Be where your feet are. What time is it? Where are you? That's the only place you can be right now."

A place you can always fill with joy.

20

Life is always on your side.

Life is always on your side. Some days I say that to myself like a mantra. Usually on those days, it's me that got in the way of whatever life was trying to teach me. I'm not always the best student.

I hate feeling powerless when life doesn't go my way. Not that my way is the best way, but I often think it is. When it isn't, I get invited by life to grow. Or to grow up. I don't usually see the opportunities until I'm caught in them, like a bug in a spider web. One time it happened during a simple trip to the dentist.

My mom needed a new dentist, so I found one close to where she lives. On the drive from my house to her assisted living apartment, I realized I calculated wrong on the time. She was 83 years old and didn't move as fast as she once did. I hadn't factored in the extra 15 minutes walking to the car in slow motion. When I called the dentist from the road, the answering machine picked up. I left a message saying we'd be late.

We arrived ten minutes late for our 10 a.m. appointment. The man behind the counter wasn't sure my mom's insurance would cover the visit even though they told me they accepted her coverage when I made the appointment.

After 15 minutes, he said her insurance was good. But we still didn't see the dentist. Meanwhile, my mom's Alzheimer's was making me squirm. With Alzheimer's, you don't just lose your memory. You can lose your edit key. I first noticed it when we were leaving the Cheesecake Factory one day and my mom commented loud enough for the people in front of us to hear, "Look at how much those people weigh! How can they eat so much?" I cringed for her and for me, but mostly for them.

Here at the dentist office, she was sitting next to an African American man. Across from her was an African American woman with three children. My mom suddenly noticed that all the people who worked at the dental office were white.

"Why don't they hire any dark-skinned people?" she said loudly.

Oh my God. Really? "Dark-skinned people?"

I knew it was the disease talking, but the man next to me didn't. I wasn't sure what to do. Maybe he didn't hear. I just hoped the people around us attributed her comments to old age. I smiled at everyone and made small talk with the children to distract my mom.

By 11 a.m., I was annoyed at the wait. When I asked how much longer, I said it loud enough for everyone in the packed waiting room to hear. I could feel people shift in their seats, and a little wave of, "Hey, what's going on here?" spread across the room. A woman got up to complain, too.

"I had a 10:30 appointment," she said. The man behind the desk got her right in.

What? Now I was angry. I approached the desk. We've been here longer, I said. The man at the desk blamed me.

"Well, you were late," he said.

"Five minutes late," I lied.

When we finally got in, the dental assistant was kind and apologized for the delay. While she took my mom to another room for X-rays, I could feel the swirl of negative energy grow in me. Some part of me wanted to be mad. I even thought about posting a negative comment on Facebook or complaining to the dentist about the man behind the desk.

Then my better angels took over. My friends in recovery long ago taught me this spiritual truth: *Anytime you're emotionally disturbed about anything, the problem is you.*

So what part of this problem was me?

As soon as I asked the question, I realized there was no problem. I got stuck waiting. Big deal. What was I "stuck" doing? The wait merely gave me more time to spend with my mom. I could look at it as a "get to" not a "have to."

Then it hit me: Most of this anger was old stuff. Childhood stuff. My past had collided with Mom's present. When we were kids, my parents sent us to the nearest dentist. He never used Novocaine when he filled a tooth. It was back before fluoride in the water, back when kids got lots of cavities. My mom went to a different dentist, so I'm not sure she ever knew the pain we endured.

He once filled five teeth in my tiny mouth without using any painkiller. It was horrifying. One time he filled a tooth and the filling fell out on the way home. I didn't tell my parents. I lived with that hole for a year. When I finally did get help, the tooth had to be pulled. It had rotted.

All these decades later, I still hate to go to a dentist. I go because I value my teeth, but I have to constantly comfort that little terrified girl inside of me when her heart starts to pound and her eyes fill with tears.

Sitting with my mom, I felt angry. Angry about that dentist she sent us to as children; angry about this one taking so long to see her. I hated hearing the drill in the other room, which made my heart race and triggered instant tears of fear.

I could climb into the past or stay present and make it better. It was all up to me. I decided to shift. To shift the focus away from being a victim of the past. To shift from being a waiting room victim forced to wait. To shift from a closed heart to an open one.

I closed my eyes and blessed the dentist, her assistant, and the man at the desk. They were all doing the best they could. I felt a trickle of peace run through me, then a stream. The shift was easy once I was willing to make it.

I meditated and sent my mom loving thoughts and told myself she did the best she could with what she had way back when we were kids. End of story. Beginning of new story. I breathed in and out as slowly as possible.

Once I entered the new story, I could see how this dentist was being extra kind to my mother. My heart softened. Until I went to pay the bill and was told I would have to wait to be called to the counter for my turn to pay.

What if the guy made me wait another hour just to punish me? No. Do not think that way, I told myself. Don't go there. Make this a "get to" moment. I "get to" spend more time with my mom.

I sat with my mom and decided to be a blessing to the people around me. I tried to fill the dental office with sparks of joy. I smiled and joked with one family and chatted with the strangers next to me.

Only a few minutes passed when the man called me up to the desk to pay. I paused and centered myself to be my best self.

"My mother had a good experience today," I told him. "The dentist and dental assistant were so kind to her." I didn't mention the long wait.

This time the man looked *at* me instead of through me. He apologized for the delay.

"I'm sure you were doing the best you could," I said, and I actually meant it.

When I took out my credit card to pay the bill, he said, "There won't be any charge today. We're running a promotion. First office visit and first X-rays are free."

He smiled. I smiled. We both knew there was no promotion. We both knew something special had happened.

We shook hands. We had both made the shift.

That brief encounter reminded me that life is on your side, once you choose to side with life.

21

If you can't hold on any longer,
God will hold on to you.

Yvonne Pointer is one of the strongest people I know. She has lived a nightmare every parent fears, one that made her a powerhouse for others.

Her oldest daughter, Gloria, was just 14 years old the last day Yvonne saw her. Gloria walked to junior high school just a few blocks away from home to receive her perfect attendance award. She never came home.

The last day Yvonne saw her, December 6, 1984, is forever etched on her soul.

That morning, Gloria got up early for school. She never missed school and was never late, so it shocked everyone when she didn't come on stage at Harry E. Davis Junior High School when they announced her name to get her award.

The principal called Yvonne. They all knew something was wrong. The school called the police.

A few hours later, police came to Yvonne's house.

"Sit down," they told her. "We found a body." Yvonne crumbled onto the floor.

Gloria had been abducted, raped, and beaten to death. When Yvonne stood by her casket, she promised, "I will find out what happened." She didn't know it would take almost 29 years.

Almost every waking moment for nearly three decades was cloaked in the question, "Who did this?"

It tormented her not to know. It cost her peace of mind for almost half of her life. But those weren't wasted years.

Yvonne worked tirelessly helping others who suffered from violent crimes. She became the hug every parent needed, the voice every family needed, the loudspeaker every neighborhood needed to combat violence all over Cleveland. She became an author, speaker, and community activist.

She turned her pain into her passion. She visited prisons, founded the Midnight Basketball program in Cleveland, mentored girls, created a scholarship fund, and built schools in Africa.

Gloria's death gave Yvonne a calling she didn't ask for. She spent the next 29 years being the voice that victims of violence needed to hear.

"When Gloria was murdered, I spent a lot of time looking for someone who would speak for me, for victims," she said. "I wrote letters and made phone calls. I was looking for myself. I just didn't realize it. My voice was the voice I was looking for."

Gloria was more than her oldest child. She was like her life partner. Yvonne had been a straight A student when she got pregnant with Gloria at 17. Back then, you didn't go to school pregnant, you had to leave. Her hopes and dreams vanished. She got her high school diploma at 24.

"We grew up together," Yvonne said. "We leaned on each other for survival."

How did her heart absorb the pain of losing Gloria? There were nights when she begged God to come get her.

One night, she couldn't take the pain anymore. She cried out, "God, please come and get me. I don't have a reason to live. Help me. I just want out."

That night, He said, "I will be your reason." He even gave her a song, "You are My Reason for Living."

Another day, she was angry at God and asked, "Do you even care about what's happening?" She went to church and cried on the altar. There, God gave her this scripture: "I am going to set the captives free."

That evening, she got a call to come to MetroHealth Medical Center in Cleveland. Three women who had been kidnapped, raped, and held captive for ten years had just escaped from a nearby home. Gina DeJesus, Amanda Berry, and Michelle Knight had been set free and taken to the closest hospital.

Yvonne rushed over and crossed the yellow police tape. A police commander told her one of the women had no family to comfort her.

"Would you sit with her?" he asked.

When Yvonne came in the emergency room, she met Michelle Knight.

"Here was this little bitty person, eyes darting back and forth," Yvonne said. "The scripture that morning had said, 'I will set the captives free and we will rejoice over them with singing'."

Yvonne didn't know what to do, so she held Michelle's hand and asked, "What is your favorite song?" Michelle told her, "Lift Every Voice and Sing." The two women sang the Black National Anthem at the top of their lungs.

She did her best to support Michelle. A few days later, the police called and asked to meet with her. At the station, an officer asked Yvonne to sit down and said, "This is not about Michelle. This is about you. We made an arrest in your daughter's case."

Yvonne sat down. The officer slid a photograph across the table. She didn't know the man.

"It's him," the officer said.

That prayer, where God told her, "I am going to set the captives free," she thought it meant Amanda, Gina, and Michelle. It turns out *Yvonne* was the one who needed to be set free.

The Cleveland police had never run the DNA collected from Gloria's murder scene back in 1984. Not until 2013, when a local reporter discovered the police had left endless DNA rape kits untested for decades.

Yvonne finally had a name: Hernandez Warren.

"Have you ever hoped for something for so long and you get it?" she said. "It's almost unbelievable."

Warren had served 16 years in prison for a rape and kidnapping in 1985. He admitted he had been high on drugs when he lured Gloria to a stairwell where he had raped and killed her.

It was hard to hear the details in the courtroom. At one point during the trial, the judge stopped and asked that Yvonne be taken out to protect her.

She did find out Gloria's last words. Gloria had called for her mother. That broke her heart.

When she did have a chance to address Gloria's killer in court, Yvonne quoted a Bible verse from Timothy: "I have fought the good fight, I have finished my course, I have kept the faith." Those words described her own journey.

She compared her life to the great American boxers.

"Ali, Smokin' Joe Frazier, I was in the ring for 29 years! I did fight a good fight. I wanted him to know I fulfilled the promise," she said. "I never stopped searching. I just didn't know it would take this long."

Then she read Genesis 49: *You meant it for evil, but God meant it for good.* She shared the good that came out the journey, that what Warren did was evil, but what God did *with it* was a gift to others.

Her last words to Warren were, "May the Lord have mercy on your soul."

And she meant it.

Warren pleaded guilty to aggravated murder and rape. He is serving life in prison with a chance of parole after 30 years.

One day Yvonne visited him in prison. She wanted to have a one-on-one meeting with him.

"I knew he'd say, 'I'm sorry.' I wanted to understand the mindset of people like him," she said.

She thought that maybe if he shared how he acted as a criminal, he might help authorities prevent child abductions and homicides.

"He cried and cried," she said. He felt sorry for himself, that he would die in prison. She told him to stop crying, grabbed his hand, and prayed.

He squeezed her fingers so hard she feared they would break. After the prayer, he said, "I just want to die. I just want to die." She told him she understood that feeling.

"I told him of the night that I had begged to die and God gave me a song," she said.

Then she sang him the song that gave her hope, "You are My

Reason for Living." She sang to him, "You are my reason for living." When she finished singing, he was crying even harder.

Yvonne said her issue most days is not with people, it's with God, who is a mystery.

"God loves the worst of us," she said, "including this person, whether I like it or not. This love was being extended toward him, and God was using me to do it."

God is still her BFF. She gives God the first 24 minutes of the day.

After all those years, it was strange no longer pursuing her daughter's killer. Now, her heart was ready to love. A woman introduced Yvonne to her brother, a gentle soul named Jerry McCreary during the pandemic. He had lost his wife of 33 years.

He and Yvonne fell in love and got married.

For the first time since Gloria's death, Yvonne could trust a man to love her, not to hurt her.

"Only you, only me, only us always," her groom told her.

And her precious Gloria, smiling in her heart forever.

22

*When the life you
chose ends, the life that
chooses you begins.*

There's no longer a rush hour in Ian Friedman's life.

Not since a medical helicopter rushed him to MetroHealth Medical Center to save his life one June day.

Not since he found himself at that place where the life you choose ends and the life that chooses you begins.

Ian is a criminal defense lawyer who was known as a bulldog and, sometimes, a bulldozer. Not anymore. He got a new grip on life after he lost the use of his arm.

One sunny day, he left his downtown Cleveland office around 6 p.m. and headed east down the Shoreway on his Harley. He took an exit, then lost control of the motorcycle. The moment he hit the guardrail and flew 100 feet has been with him every day since June 17, 2011. He calls it the best thing that happened to him.

He flew off the motorcycle and skidded across a rusty guardrail. All 100 feet of it. Each post of the guardrail ripped into him. It nearly severed his thumb. The metal tore into his neck and severed the nerves in his arm. You could see the bones in his spine. It barely missed slicing his aorta and spinal cord. He broke a leg, shoulder, and collarbone. His broken ribs punctured his lung.

He closed his eyes and asked God, "Am I going to die? Is this my time?"

All he heard was silence.

When he opened his eyes, he heard these words: "It's OK to get up and walk and be happy."

The sun was still shining. The sky was still blue. He was still here.

Lucky for him, among the strangers who stopped were two doctors. He remembers every police officer, paramedic, and stranger giving him their very best.

At Hillcrest Hospital, his friend Joe Delguyd held his good hand.

"You're OK, you're OK," Joe lied.

Surgeons at MetroHealth closed the gash in his neck and saved his thumb. They installed a metal rod to repair his leg. They discovered the guardrail had ripped out five vital nerves in his arm.

Ian's left arm is paralyzed. It dangles dead at his side when he's not wearing his black arm sling. He has to be careful not to burn it or catch it in a door. Horrible phantom pains run from his elbow to his fingers like a hot sword. He's grateful to be right-handed and for the help he's found online at the United Brachial Plexus Network to cope with his injuries.

"People just adjust," he said. "I tied my tie this morning. I saw on YouTube how to do it. There's a way to do everything. I kind of like the challenge."

Ian went to the Mayo Clinic where surgeons took nerves from his chest to implant in his arm and transfer muscle from his leg into his shoulder area. He hopes to regain some function.

For now, everything is slower, more deliberate. Buttoning the cuff on his right wrist is tough. So is tying his shoes. He's had to figure out how to close the car door, deal with drive-through windows, and ask strangers for help.

Having the use of just one arm has slowed down and deepened his life. It takes a lot longer to shave, button a shirt, and tie a shoe. Instead of finding it awkward to hug with one arm, his hugs are stronger than ever because of the person he has become. He's grateful for the fresh canvas he got for the second half of his life and talks about what to write on it if you get one.

The accident changed him as an attorney. When you're a criminal defense attorney, you often see the grisly underbelly of life.

"Now I see the very best in people every single day," he said.

He's now managing partner of Friedman, Nemecek, Long & Grant, LLC, in Cleveland and owner of First Strike Indoor Range, where people can learn how to safely handle guns.

His goal as an attorney is to treat his clients as if they were members of his own family, to stand up for them, and to work hard to protect their rights and freedom. He's known for successfully taking on cases that were seen as unwinnable.

Cleveland State University gave Ian a Distinguished Alumni award. The Ohio Association of Criminal Defense Lawyers gave him its first annual Lawyer of the Year award. Ian worked with the Ohio Prosecuting Attorneys Association and the Ohio Supreme Court to make Ohio's discovery practice in criminal law more open and fairer.

Ian is humbled by both awards but more by his new life, one that includes a new marriage and children.

"I smell things differently and see things for the first time. I was given a fresh canvas for the second half of my life. What's important to me is completely different. I'm a better friend, a better father, a better lawyer."

He believes the biggest crime in life is wasted time.

"The arm, it's crazy, but it's the best thing that's ever happened to me. I love having this reminder 24/7. That left arm sits there and keeps everything in perspective. I can't fall back into the grind."

Every day, it's enough to simply get up, walk, and be happy.

23

You deserve to be taken care of by somebody, and that somebody is you.

French fashion designer Coco Chanel once said, "The most courageous act is still to think for yourself. Aloud."

But don't just think for yourself; *do* for yourself.

Loudly and boldly.

I once read an article by Paulette Perhach about why every woman should have an emergency fund. She called it an FOF, a F--- Off Fund, in case you have to flee a job, an apartment, or a relationship.

Or you could call it something more nurturing, like an IDB Fund: I Deserve Better.

One of my sisters calls it her "Go to hell" money. She once had to confront a vice president at work about inappropriate sexual comments. He got huffy, but she stood strong. Unfortunately, she got the lowest annual increase in the entire company that year. She was the compensation manager, so she knew what everyone made. All these years later, she's still glad she spoke up.

It's easier to speak up if you have money to back you up. Thank goodness she had some.

My dad used to slip us twenty dollars all the time. He didn't say why, but we knew. I still try to keep an extra twenty dollars in my wallet. You never know when you will need cab fare, bus fare, or a meal. Remember all those movies where women slipped money into their bra? Yep. That was their self-defense fund.

Somewhere in my 30s life taught me that a man is not a financial plan. I was engaged to a man I thought was my future. While I was looking at fairy-tale wedding dresses, Prince Charming was sleeping around. That's when I got my act together and went back to college to get my degree so I could create a better living and have better choices, including the choice to walk away from a guy who cheats.

Even if you're married, you need to have a bank account in your own name and a support system that will support you through a divorce or the death of your partner.

After reading Paulette's article, I made a list of the basic survival skills every woman needs to know to fend for herself:

First, every time you walk out the door, bring your ID, cash, house key, and a charged cell phone with the emergency medical information filled out in that little white app with the red heart.

Other must haves: a valid passport, a decent piece of luggage, and an education. Get your high school diploma or GED, then finish that bachelor's degree.

Have a credit card in your name. Preferably one you pay off every month. If not, that Coach purse you got on sale wasn't really on sale if you're paying interest on it.

When it comes to travel, you need to know how to . . .

Check in for a flight.

Hail a cab.

Read a map, use Google maps, and a GPS.

Fix a bike flat.

Tip a server, a cab driver, and a hotel housekeeper—every night.

If you own a car, always have . . .

At least a half tank of gas in the car. I love that country music lyric, "There's a half a tank of freedom in my Chevy and I'm leavin'."

The magic of an AAA card, unless you know someone to give you a tow at 2 a.m.

A secret stash of quarters for parking meters to avoid parking tickets.

Car insurance and proof of it in your wallet.

A Life Hammer in the console to smash a window or cut a seatbelt to rescue you or someone else.

A tire gauge to check the tire pressure.

A first aid kit and flashlight with batteries that actually work.

Learn how to jump-start a car battery, check the oil, fill the wiper fluid, and, yes, change a tire.

Never ever, ever drive drunk. If you plan to drink, plan your ride home before you pick up the first margarita.

Before you move into your own a home, know how to . . .

Unclog a drain. Free a clogged toilet with a plunger.

Safely use a fireplace.

Use a hammer and a drill.

Know the difference between a flat head and Phillips screw-driver.

Assemble anything. (Read the directions. Check to see all parts and needed tools are present. Read the directions again.)

Free or kill a spider, bee, or mouse in the house.

Always have a roll of duct tape and a can of WD-40. Something always needs tightened or loosened.

Learn to change a fuse, paint a room, and move furniture without getting hurt. (Lift from the legs, not the back, and slide it on a towel across a wood floor.)

Money gives you choices and freedom.
Make sure you can . . .

Do your own taxes or have your own accountant.

Know the value of compound interest.

Set a budget.

Balance a checkbook.

Pay yourself first and set aside 10 percent for retirement now because it matters more now than when you're older. (See the value of compounding.)

Understand the limits and consequences of a debit card and a credit card.

Open a checking account, savings account, and retirement fund in your name.

Protect your privacy settings and passwords online.

Recognize scammers, and never click on a link allegedly sent from a friend without making sure they sent it.

Figure out how to get health insurance.

If any financial transaction doesn't feel right and you don't clearly understand ALL the details and fine print, do NOT say yes to any financial planner, investment, time share, life insurance, or loan.

When it comes to work, know how to . . .

Negotiate your incoming salary *before* taking the job. Women earn less than men for the same work because they START at a lower salary.

Ask for a meaningful, significant raise.

Quit a job without burning any bridges.

Give yourself a pep talk in a restroom stall.

Find a mentor, learn from criticism, and know when to ask for help.

Tie a tie. Tie a scarf at least three ways.

Remove red wine, chocolate, and olive oil from a shirt.

Sew a button on a shirt, hem a pair of slacks, iron a blouse.

Use LinkedIn, Twitter, Facebook, Instagram, and TikTok.

To experience joy with others, know how to . . .

Ask someone out. Break up gracefully.

Decline texting pictures or sending videos of your private areas to anyone. Ever.

Say *no*. Practice saying it loudly and often.

Respect *no* when someone else says it, even if it's softly.

Contact three BFFs in case you lose your cell phone and need to be rescued from a bad date, a rocky marriage, or a rough night of drinking.

Make an impromptu toast.

Use the correct fork at a fancy dinner.

Set a table correctly.

Write a thank-you note by hand and mail it.

Apologize. (Never say, I'm sorry if I hurt you. Name exactly what you did and apologize for it using the words, "I'm sorry.")

Accept a compliment. Instead of diminishing it or ignoring it, simply say, "Thank you."

Use Uber or a similar ride app on your cell phone.

For basic survival skills, be able to . . .

Perform CPR, the Heimlich maneuver. and stop bleeding.

Create an emergency shelter in the wilderness.

Cook one meal without a recipe. Know how to use recipes.

Make a signature cocktail, a great dessert, and assemble an appetizer with whatever you have in the fridge.

Hard boil an egg.

Cook rice.

Choose the right wine and open it without a fancy cork-screw.

Use a barbecue grill, gas or with coals, and grill a burger well enough so no one dies from E. coli.

For fun, you might want to know . . .

One card trick, a magic trick, and a yoga pose.

An amazing cookie recipe.

A song from memory to play on the piano, guitar, or harmonica.

How to ride a bike. Fly a kite. Shuffle a deck of cards.

Being prepared for anything doesn't mean you hate men or expect the worst from others or live as if the world is out to get you.

It means you're ready to meet any challenge. You might

always have great friends and family to rely on, but if you don't, you still have somebody looking out for you.

You.

24

Choose to survive.

It was supposed to be the trip of a lifetime, a three-week vacation to get away and get her life back on track.

Sophie Sureau was successful but wasn't happy. She lived in São Paulo, Brazil, with her boyfriend, and her corporate job left little time for sleep. She was exhausted, burned out, and drowning in anxiety. She was 35 but making poor choices, like staying out late having too much fun with work colleagues.

The plan was to take three weeks off in Southeast Asia. They would hit Hong Kong, then Malaysia, then the island of Borneo. She thought the trip would change everything.

It did, but not in the way she could ever imagine.

The second week of the trip, she and her boyfriend, Jeff, headed to Indonesia to the island of Bali for rest and relaxation. They arrived on a Friday to get settled in and scope out where to rent a car. On Saturday, they planned to enjoy the pool and the beach, but the sky was gray, so they got familiar with the area and found a restaurant for the night.

Around 4 p.m., friends joined them around the pool to plan their first evening in Bali. They were standing around a small dance floor in an open-air bar with music blasting. The area was filled with Westerners, most of them from Australia and Europe, in town for a rugby tournament.

Sophie was standing in a circle of friends that had just ordered their first drink when, BOOM! The Irish pub across the street blew up. It was the first bar they were going to go to but decided not to.

Sophie had a quick thought of relief, then suddenly, BOOM! The second bomb exploded a few feet away from her.

That day, Saturday, October 12, 2002, a terrorist group affiliated with Al-Qaeda killed 202 people and injured 300.

Sophie lost consciousness. She was burned and buried under rubble. She regained consciousness when she felt people walking on her back to escape the carnage. She was pinned under debris, broken tables, chairs, and pieces of the roof. She tried to get up but couldn't. People were walking on her to flee the flames.

She felt the flames lick her arm and back. Her face felt on fire. And then it kicked in: the adrenaline to survive. Her choice was to burn to death or get up. She felt as if she turned herself into a superhero to survive, fleeing the scene with skin hanging from her body.

For a minute she couldn't hear anything. The deafening sound of the explosion had perforated her eardrums. Skin hung from her arms. Her feet were bleeding.

She didn't know where to go, but she knew this: "I need to get out of here, and I need to survive." The pain she was feeling wasn't her top priority. Fleeing the scene to survive was.

Her life flashed before her in black and white, like a movie from her childhood to the birth of her niece, who had just turned six months old.

"I had not met her yet," she told me. "That was the image that got me going. I decided, I'm getting up for my family."

That was the moment she chose to survive.

"I completely believe that was the moment for me. Am I going to stay here and burn to death, or am I going to get up and live?"

She remembers that moment of choice: "I remember getting up as if I were the Incredible Hulk, like, *Get out of my way! I'm going to survive this.* I felt like I was big and green."

Fight *and* flight kicked in.

She saw a man and woman on a scooter and asked the woman to get off so the man could take her to the nearest hospital. There, she saw two construction trucks filled with bodies. Some were moving; some were not. She walked in and realized they were too overwhelmed to help. The man drove her to another hospital, and finally to a third where she could be treated.

Once she was cleaned up and bandaged up, the physical pain hit. It went on for months. She had endless surgeries, rehabilitation, and therapy sessions. She had suffered third-degree burns over 23 percent of her body. She spent 35 days in a Singapore hospital and had to have skin grafts.

All these years later, two moments stand out from the bombing: the moment she chose to survive, and the moment she knew that her boyfriend had survived.

When Jeff couldn't find her in the fire, he thought she was dead. He saved others that day, even though he was burned over 9 percent of his body. He spent that night grieving her death.

The next morning, when she saw him in the hospital, she knew: This is my husband. In that moment, it felt like they were instantly married. He stayed and helped nurse her to health.

At the hospital, when she was able to walk again, she visited patients burned worse than her. In physical therapy and in occupational therapy, she became a cheerleader for others, encouraging them to push harder to regain use of their arms, hands, and legs.

"I remember the first time I was able to eat on my own in the hospital, bringing a fork or spoon to my mouth without having someone feed me. It was amazing," she said.

Her body is scarred for life, but she has made those scars her gift.

"Looking at myself in the mirror every day is a reminder that I'm lucky," she said. "I'm lucky to be here, and I need to make the most of it."

She no longer works in the corporate world making money for shareholders. Now she focuses on making a difference. Sophie, another patient, and a physician started the nonprofit Helping Hands for Burn Survivors in Montreal. In her coaching and mentoring, she helps people make the tough decisions they need to make to propel their lives forward.

I met her when she worked for Susan G. Komen for the Cure in Cleveland to give hope to breast cancer survivors like me. I love that Sophie refuses to be called a victim. She chooses to live as a survivor and warrior.

Once you decide to survive, you choose to own your scars. You worked too hard to save your life to be bothered by them. In time, you don't feel like a victim. You feel like a warrior.

She and Jeff did get married. They have two children. Sophie works at Case Western Reserve University in Cleveland, where she helps donors maximize the impact of their dollars, doing things like raising money for first-time college students.

She's religious about taking care of her body. She wakes at 5:30 a.m., meditates, drinks a large glass of water, then goes for a 45-minute walk to get her 10,000 steps in before anyone else wakes up, or she makes her way to yoga.

Her secret? Get to bed by ten and wear your workout clothes to sleep. She says, "I dress for tomorrow."

Her scars remind her of the person she once was and the powerful survivor she is today.

"Every day is a battle in all of our lives," she said. "You have to choose to win those battles."

And winning starts with the choice to survive.

25

Fear is a big fat liar.

My dad took on the world from the back of a B-24 bomber. He tucked all six feet of himself in the rear of the plane, hunkered down, and blasted away.

"Pow, pow, pow, pow, pow, pow, pow," he used to say as he pumped his fists to show us how. He was the tallest tail gunner in the 24th Combat Mapping Squadron. He chose the dangerous duty of a tail gunner because it paid more, and his family back home needed the money.

Staff Sgt. Thomas A. Brett was fearless. He flew more than 30 missions in the China Burma Theater of War. Then he came back to his small town in Ohio and raised us to be afraid of life.

Everything could and would hurt us. Branches that hung too low could poke your eye out. A rubber band flying off a finger could blind you. Sitting too close to the TV would weaken your eyes. Keeping your hands in your pockets could prove fatal if you tripped and couldn't break your fall.

And don't even think about riding in a snowmobile (head injury) or going in the ocean (drowning) or riding in a compact car (certain death).

My dad had a safety plan for everything, including a thick rope tied to the end of our bedpost. We were instructed to toss the rope out of our second-floor window and climb out to escape a fire.

Dad taught us to be afraid of the world. It turned out, for me, the scariest person to trust back then was him. I still sleep with my ears covered with a sheet to block out the creak of his feet on the steps. I hated the sound of his belt and someone crying from being hit. That one step always gave him away so I could pretend to be asleep.

Every time I hear Reba McIntyre sing, "Because of You," the words haunt me: "Because of you I never stray too far from the sidewalk. Because of you I learned to play on the safe side so I don't get hurt ... Because of you I am afraid."

We were taught to stay on our side of Sycamore Street. We had to ask to cross the street until we were in high school, yet we were allowed to play baseball and football in the middle of the street. Go figure.

I still fear authority figures will take away everything I'm looking forward to right at the last minute. I still push people away before they have the chance to hurt or disappoint me. I still hear those warnings from my childhood, *The world is not a safe place. Be careful. Stay close to home. Family comes first. Family will protect you.*

What if your family was the greatest danger of all?

You have no one.

At least that's what it felt like when I cried alone in the apple tree, in the laundry pile, or in my bed at night rocking myself to sleep.

I grew up scared of life.

Fear still makes way too many of my choices. Even what to wear: Will this dress be too sexy or make me look too feminine and vulnerable and invite an attack? Can I run in these shoes if I had to get away?

I keep the car locked while driving and the house locked while in it.

People might call it anxiety. Nope, it's straight-up fear.

One day I heard a woman suggest that we give fear an expiration date, so I did. It helped for a while, but the fear crept back in.

I once read that bravery is when you're the only one who knows you are afraid, so I read books on brave women, like Marie Curie, Rosa Parks, and Joan of Arc, who heard the voice of God at 13 and followed it all the way to the stake at 19.

I chip away at the iceberg of fear, at least the part I can see sticking out of the water, so it doesn't run my life aground. As much as I want it all removed, it hasn't all melted, but a big chunk floated away in Maine after I attended a Self-Care by the Sea retreat held by author Cheryl Richardson in the spring of 2017.

At one point, she asked all the women in the room to share our answers to this question: "If I knew that everything would turn out okay, I would change _____ in my life."

Geez, I'd change everything.

I would walk to my car without the fear of being attacked. I would keep the windows open in my house without the fear of finding a stranger in the closet. I would try new hobbies without the fear of doing them wrong or getting hurt. I would be more authentic and speak my truth. I would spend more time in nature hiking without being afraid of wild animals and men.

I would risk being famous and not fear losing my privacy. I'd eat more ice cream without fear of having a stroke in my 80s. I'd write all the books in me without the bogey man of my family editing over my shoulders. I'd travel more often without fear of losing my luggage or getting lost.

I would trust life more. I would *love* life more—and I already love it a lot.

When I told the group of women that I had a chronic fear that life would hurt me, Cheryl asked me to describe that fear, then told me to close my eyes.

Listen within and pick a number, she said.

Five.

That's the age you were, she said. Then she asked me to close my eyes, take a few deep breaths, and share an image, word, sound, scent that came to that five-year-old me.

It happened so fast I ducked.

"Me ducking," I said. "So I don't get hit."

Cheryl asked the room, "Did you just see her duck?" They all did.

She asked for more information. "Who hit you?"

My dad. My first-grade teacher. My third-grade teacher.

"You've spent your whole life ducking from life," she said.

Bingo.

I am still ducking from my dad's belt and mom's angry silence and Sister Peter's wooden paddle and Sister Dolores' book smacking me on the head.

On the retreat, I decided to get counseling to help me stop ducking. That's not what I want to model for my grandchildren, a life diminished by fear.

Before I left the retreat, I stood on the balcony outside my room and cried one last good cry. Every cry now is a good cry because I'm willing to feel the pain and sadness behind and underneath all that fear. When I looked below, I saw ducks cavorting and splashing in the harbor outside my window.

Ducks.

They would dunk, disappear, then pop up a few feet away, flap their wings in applause, swim a few feet away, and repeat the fun. My tears turned to laughter. I got the message.

Life was letting me know it was time to stop ducking.

It was time to start diving in.

26

You are never alone.
God is right where you are.

Sometimes you don't see the sadness coming and life flattens you in an instant, like a hit-and-run you never saw coming.

I was sailing along, buying groceries at the Giant Eagle to fill my mother's fridge in her memory unit apartment with apples, grapes, Diet Coke, and sugar-free pudding.

She was down in the dining hall when I stopped at her room. The little bowl of salted nuts on the counter startled me. She had given up nuts for Lent, and I kept forgetting and bringing her a new can every visit. Her cupboard was full of canned nuts. Somehow, I kept forgetting, yet somehow my mother with Alzheimer's never forgot. Until now.

I wrote "Regina Was Here" in her daily calendar book and drew a big smiley face so she wouldn't forget. But she would. She would forget I brought her the flowers. She would forget I stopped by on Friday.

At least she still remembered who I was.

I am her daughter. Sort of. I morphed into her errand girl, bill payer, complaint taker, problem solver, personal shopper, and ride to the dentist.

The truth is, I've never felt like anyone's daughter. Not really.

When I opened her fridge and saw it was empty, my heart sank. She did receive three meals a day, but also liked having a full fridge of her favorite items. She was out of milk and pop and grapes. I had been too busy to stop by earlier in the week. When I'm torn between the bookends of life, I choose the future and visit my grandkids.

Mom had run out of bathroom tissue and her Poise pads and was using the thin brand the facility provided. I always bring her the extra soft kind. I felt so guilty and sad, that I had neglected her most basic needs. The living facility supplied tissue and pads, but they aren't the softest kind. I wanted her to have the best.

I walked down to the common dining room and couldn't find her. All the women seem to look the same: white hair, part of them present, part of them somewhere else. Then I heard her laugh. I pulled up a chair next to her. She grinned and hugged me, poked at her egg salad, then said we should go to her room.

There we had the same three conversations we always had:

LeBron James: *They were going to give him a parade in Cleveland, but he said,* I'm from Akron and never lived in Cleveland, *so they gave him a parade in Akron.*

The Best Day of Her Life: *I had an argument with my father, and I finally let him have it. I told him off good. It was the best day of my life.*

This Place is Full of Old People: *I'm the youngest one here. I don't belong here. They're all 90 or 100. Some of them don't remember their own names.*

I nodded and always acted surprised, like it was the first time

I'd heard about LeBron or her dad or the old folks around her. She was 84, the average age of the residents.

There was no point changing the subject. For a while, I could lift the needle on the record and move it to another conversation, but the groove was worn so deep that it kept skipping. It used to be that only part of the record skipped. Now the whole record that is Mom skipped.

When I left her with big hugs and wishes for a happy Easter, she walked me to the locked door. She used to sneak and learn the code. Not anymore. She forgot to do it. She forgot what freedom felt like.

My heart sank seeing her grin and wave goodbye like a child. I thought about that change of address card my brother made her that read, *Mother of 11 waiting on heaven.* What was God waiting for? she often asked me. I asked on days when I saw another piece of her slip away.

I stopped by the chapel. It was just a few feet from the memory unit's locked door. The light was on. The little red light that says *Jesus Is Home.* Catholic school taught me that light meant the Eucharist is present in the chapel. It was a real candle, not a fake electric glow that some churches plug in.

No one was in the chapel, but the light felt like an invitation, so I walked up to the altar. A large crucifix rested on it from the Good Friday service. Catholic instinct took over. I bent down and kissed the feet of Jesus.

Then I sat in a chair. No, I pretty much crumbled into it and started to cry.

God take her home, I prayed. God take my mother home. She wants to go. And I want her to go before she forgets who we are, forgets who she is.

What a terrible prayer, yet the most honest one in me.

I looked around to make sure no one heard me. It was just me and the deep blue and red shards of stained glass that made up an entire wall behind the altar. The darkness that held those bricks of light together seemed to understand.

Then suddenly I saw it.

Now, I had been in this chapel at least a dozen times and passed by it more times than I could count. And never had I ever seen it before:

There, built into the stained-glass window, was a huge stained-glass dove.

Not a small, itty-bitty bird. A stained-glass dove with the wingspan of an eagle. It had been there forever. How had I never noticed?

A friend of mine says, "You know when you've been 'doved'." It's that moment God's presence is so clear, it's like God used a sledgehammer or a billboard to drive home the point, but God is more graceful than that and sends a dove.

I had been doved.

I still felt sad. But I wasn't alone in my sadness.

The spiritual writer Ernest Holmes wrote, "God is not separate from what He is doing. The Divine Life is in everyone and in everything. This is the secret . . . God is right where you are."

Even if it isn't where you want to be.

27

The magic is tucked right there in the mess.

Life is messy.

Every mom knows that. We also know that magic is tucked right there in the mess.

Through the pandemic, life was even messier. The coronavirus turned parents into teachers overnight. On top of fixing breakfast, lunch, and dinner, doing laundry, looking for missing socks, going off to work, or staying home to complete a thousand other chores, moms (and some dads) had to teach science, reading, and math.

I'm amazed at how well my daughter adapted overnight to teaching her three kids, who were 6, 8, and 11 during the start of the pandemic. She turned the family room into a classroom, complete with wipe boards, lesson plans, and stacks of books.

Parenthood is full of detours. You over-prepare, then go with the flow. Some days it's a trickle, some days, a flood that threatens to drown everybody. It feels like we're all treading water. We're all doing the best we can on any given day.

My gramma did the best she could, even though she could

never read or write English. An immigrant from Czechoslovakia, she raised five children on a farm and earned money cleaning houses.

My mom did the best she could, even though we outnumbered her 11 to 1. I did the best I could, even though I was a single mom who worked full time for 18 years.

My daughter is doing the best she can, so much better than I ever did, even when she had to serve as a teaching assistant to all three.

Most every parent is doing the best they can. Most days, that best is a moving target, as it was during the global pandemic. I laughed every time someone posted a Facebook message, like: "Home schooling is going well. Two students suspended for fighting and one teacher fired for drinking on the job."

Or, "If you see my kids locked outside today, mind your business. We are having a fire drill."

And this: "If you see my kids crying outside and picking weeds, just keep on driving. It's just a field trip."

We tried to create a Covid-19 Daily Routine to harness the crazy, but the chaos stampeded all over it. I saw one humorous post with an original schedule listing things like, Wake up, Morning time, Academic time, Creative time, Chore time, and so on. I was tempted to send it to my daughter until I noticed the column next to it: "Woken up by kid in your face saying sibling said shut up . . . Everyone cries . . . Spill glitter . . . Cry again . . . Count how many times kids ask you when quiet time is over."

Yes, everyone will cry. Even you.

Yes, there will be glitter everywhere. And gum. And crushed Cheerios.

And those damn LEGOs attacking your feet every step of the way.

And one day, all of that mess will be over. All of this chaos and craziness will be the memories you laugh over and the stories you tell and the gifts that made you stronger.

That plus sign you saw all those years ago on that pregnancy stick? It meant baby plus everything else. Madness and messes and magic and mystery.

That's what makes parenting so challenging and fulfilling, so awful and so awesome. You really wouldn't want it any other way, would you?

Even if you do hear your home-schooled child say, "I hope I don't get the same teacher next year."

Yes, there is magic everywhere. Even in the mess. Especially in the mess.

Every year I watch countless Hallmark movies featuring the perfect Christmas. One of our best Christmas holidays was one of the messiest.

We always decorate our Christmas tree the day after Thanksgiving. That's our tradition. And we fill it full of memories: the glued pasta cardboard wreath my daughter made when she was three. Her first pair of mittens, pink with no thumbs. A pine cone covered in glitter. She used to roll her eyes, but now she's in her 40s and has three children of her own, so she knows those are the most important ornaments. The homemade messy kind.

Then there are the glamorous ones. My husband's brother buys us Waterford crystal ornaments that have elevated the art of decorating our tree. They're stunning when the angel, the stocking, and the wreath catch the miniature lights and spread glittery light all over the room.

When we finished decorating, the tree looked glorious.

Then someone hid the Christmas pickle, a fragile green ornament shaped like a dill pickle. It's a German tradition to hide one. Whoever finds it wins a gift. In our house, it's a chocolate coin.

I was standing in the living room admiring the tree when CRASH! It came apart and seemed to have broken in half and crashed to the wood floor. Standing beneath the tree, actually standing *in* the tree, was my six-year-old granddaughter. She was covered in shattered ornaments.

"Don't move!" we shouted, afraid she'd be sliced up if she took a step or a breath.

As we gently air-lifted her away from the tree, she kept crying, "I'm sorry. I'm sorry. I'm sorry. I couldn't find the Christmas pickle."

I think in her magical eyes, it was a real tree that she tried to climb to get to the pickle.

All day the tree stood forlorn until we ran to the store to buy a replacement for the tree stand, which had been damaged in the fall. While we were at the store, my daughter called and told us to leave and head straight home. We did, and when we pulled in the drive, the Christmas tree looked as stunning as ever, lit up and standing tall in one piece. No mess. Just magic. My daughter had sneaked over with her own tree stand, righted the tree, and redecorated it.

"It's a Christmas miracle!" we all joked.

And in some ways, it was.

Out of all the perfect Hallmark Christmas holidays we've had, this will likely be the one we remember and cherish the most. The year the tree broke. The year the ornaments crashed. The year we didn't care how the tree looked because the little girl who believed in Santa and Christmas pickle magic was okay.

She never did find the pickle. Her brother, who was 10 at the time, hid it so well that no one found it. Until the day we took down the tree.

After I removed every single ornament, as I pulled off the last branch, I heard a tinkling sound, almost like a bell as it fell. Did an angel just get its wings? Perhaps.

The pickle landed gently onto the soft red skirt still tucked around the tree. Not a scratch on it. It looked like a big green smile.

I smiled back. Yes, that pickle will go on the tree next year and every year.

28

Each of us is a divine mystery worth celebrating.

The man was a mystery.

I still think of him whenever I visit my alma mater.

Anyone who ever lived in Kent, Ohio, or went to school at Kent State University during a certain era had an encounter with him, often a disturbing or confusing one.

Most people didn't know his name, so they wouldn't have connected the dots when the local newspaper reported that Robert E. Wood died.

Most people knew him as F.U. Bob. He was the man who stood at intersections all over Kent holding up his middle finger to the world.

He looked wild and disheveled, with a long, narrow face and an even longer scraggly beard that looked like an unraveled Brillo pad. He stepped around sidewalk cracks and climbed up and down the same curb over and over before crossing a street. He dropped the F-bomb without warning or provocation, and his explosive outbursts angered and scared people.

But he was so much more than that obscene gesture, than

the crude words he uttered, than all those quirks that were perhaps a neurological disorder or a form of mental illness. We just didn't know it.

Robert Wood was an artist.

Most of what I learned about him came after he died. He flipped me off regularly since I lived in Kent for 11 years. I did my best to stay out of the line of fire. I wasn't aware of his art until my friend Judy called me just before my daughter got married. Judy said she was going to buy the newlyweds one of F.U. Bob's paintings as a wedding gift. She said he had done a series of fog paintings. Or at least that's what I heard on the phone. Sure, I said.

Turns out it was a series of *frog* paintings. It turned out to be a gorgeous piece of work in purples and greens that graces a special place in their home.

Robert had a master's degree in painting from Kent State and won awards for his work. He was constantly sketching life from a bar, park bench, or church pew. He was originally from Youngstown, Ohio, and came to Kent in the 1960s. He worked in paint, watercolors, and markers and won many art awards.

The man who ran the local art gallery knew Robert for 15 years.

"He had a complex personality," the owner said. "Sometimes it's hard to tell the difference between the idiot and the savant."

He had a hard time selling Robert's work because Robert's personality got in the way. Like many, he was stunned at the crowd at the memorial. Nearly 200 people packed the Unitarian Universalist Church of Kent that Saturday morning in 2012.

Robert was like a folk hero to them.

At the memorial, the gallery owner read an essay Robert

wrote called, *Concerning the spiritual in art*: "Creativity is empowering, giving one a measure of self-control . . . What is art then if not spiritual?"

Robert seemed to be an expert on everything—philosophy, politics, music, films, art history, mythology, and health. Even though he lived in Kent for over 50 years, he didn't consider himself a townie. He called himself a tourist. He always saw the world he lived in as brand new.

His greatest gift wasn't his art; it was how he made peace with a world that didn't fit. Robert spent Sunday evenings at a local church working on his art. The pastor there spoke directly to him at the memorial.

"I loved that about you, Robert," the pastor said. "You made uncomfortable beautiful."

Was Robert Wood brilliant or was he ill?

Robert taught us that you can be both.

Almost every town has a Robert, someone that stands out for the wrong reasons, for his odd behavior, dress or demeanor, yet inside possesses a vibrant soul. Too often it's lost under the label we give them: homeless, mentally ill, or worse, bum, crazy. The truth is, they make the fabric of the community richer by adding their frayed texture.

College towns often attract the curious and eclectic. Kent was famous for the tragedy of May 4, 1970, when the Ohio National Guard fired into a crowd of students protesting the Vietnam War. Four students were killed and nine injured. It took decades for the town and university to recover. The wounded town seemed to attract wounded souls. It was, and is, a place where you can blend in with the other eccentrics, where the misfits can fit.

It turns out Robert had many friends who offered him rides or a place to shower. He ate free hot meals at local churches yet was known to donate his own groceries to a needy family. One on one, Robert engaged in intellectual debates with those who saw past his gruff exterior, who discovered his beautiful mind.

When I lived in Kent, people wanted to know what was wrong with him. He had a sort of strange cult following that never solved the riddle that was Robert: Was his brain damaged from drugs? Did he have Tourette's syndrome? Did he suffer from bipolar disorder? Schizophrenia?

I'm not sure anyone ever knew for sure. I worried for him every new school year that the next batch of incoming fresh-men wouldn't be so forgiving of his outbursts and might hurt him, especially on weekends when the beer flowed so freely from the bars on Water Street.

At some point, Robert must have gotten medical help, or embracing his art softened him. Over the years, his behavior grew less erratic, and his art grew more popular. He socialized more; he was seen at summer chamber concerts and plays. He started sharing his paintings and drawings with the public and sold them at the farmer's market and local art fairs.

The manager of the social service agency where Robert came for hot meals wrote this when she heard he died of a heart attack at age 68:

"Perhaps eccentric people are incarnations of God, for they challenge us to look deeper for their divinity, which is masked by behaviors that put them at the margins of society. Robert did, indeed, challenge this community to look beyond the gruff exterior for his hidden talents and wisdom.

"The word 'grace' is defined as undeserved blessings from

God. My minister, Rev. Melissa Carvill-Ziemer, points out that in modeling God's example, some people, more than others, require us to work harder at extending grace to them because they evoke fear in us . . . sometimes loving someone takes courage."

Melissa told me everyone who had the courage to love Robert learned something from him.

"He knew more about how to see people as people than a lot of us do," she said.

The man was both a mystery and a masterpiece.

But then, aren't we all?

29

Depression lies. Don't listen.

Depression lies.

It tells you that you aren't worthy of help. It tells you that life will hurt you if you leave the house. It tells you dying is better than living. It tells you no one can save you.

Depression killed my cousin's daughter. It killed two of my husband's cousins. It killed his brother-in-law on Christmas Eve.

It kills famous people, too, people who seem to have everything to live for. Depression doesn't care. It killed Kate Spade, Robin Williams, Anthony Bourdain, Kurt Cobain, and Naomi Judd.

You can have all the success in the world, a family who loves you, a great job that supports you, but depression tells you something else. It tells you you're a failure. It tells you that you'll never feel better. It tells you you're a burden on your family. It covers you in a darkness no light or love can penetrate.

Sadly, people don't get it. After actor Robin Williams died, people were baffled. How could such a funny guy with so much fame, money, and talent kill himself?

Depression doesn't care what your income is. It doesn't care what kind of house you have or where your kids go to school or how happy or unhappy your marriage is.

Depression doesn't care that your children have their whole lives ahead of them and that they need you to be in their future.

Depression is a complex, complicated, medical condition. It is not a character flaw or a weakness or a result of bad choices.

Those lies it tells you are cognitive distortions. They are part of the illness. They will grow louder and last longer if your depression is untreated. It's the disease that is telling you no one will understand, that all is lost, that the world is better off without you, that death is the only way to end the pain for everyone.

Depression will lie and say medicine won't help. The truth is antidepressants have saved countless lives.

Depression will lie and tell you no one knows your pain. The truth is there are support groups everywhere and great psychotherapists who can help.

Depression will lie and tell you there is no hope. The truth is depression is a treatable illness.

Depression will lie and tell you suicide will end the pain. It doesn't tell you that it will cause a lifetime of pain to every single person you leave behind.

There is help. I have many loved ones who suffer from depression and got help. My friend Danielle Wiggins publicly shared her journey with depression.

She grew up in Bedford, Ohio, and had big dreams when she went off to the University of Missouri–Columbia. She wanted to be a TV news anchor and a reporter. She was doing well until her second year and even pledged a sorority. When she went home for spring break, everything was fine.

When she returned to college, depression hit. She could barely talk. She shook all the time.

"Mom took me to the hospital. I was diagnosed with clinical depression," she said. "I didn't want to accept it. I didn't want to believe it.

"In my little 19-year-old mind, my life fell apart," she said. "I thought of the word 'crazy.' In the black community, you don't get depressed. Nobody gets depressed. They tell you, 'Go to church! You have to be strong.' It was very, very hard for me to recover from that."

She took an incomplete in most of her classes because her mother took her home for the summer for treatment.

"Outwardly, I was upset," she said. "Inside, my soul was rejoicing. I was on a terrible road, and they were there to save me. My mom knew I couldn't survive by myself. I needed a lot more help."

She worked part-time, took classes at the local community college, but spent most of the day in bed.

In the fall, she returned to college, but the symptoms grew more severe. She stopped going to class and was afraid to leave her dorm room. She had been a straight A student until thoughts of fear flooded her brain and made her afraid to get out of bed. She slept all day to avoid life, which wasn't like her. She was typically energetic.

"I was just afraid of people," she said. "I felt a failure. I couldn't do anything right. It was terrible. I wanted to sleep all day to avoid whatever I had to face.

"I needed to be perfect. It was my mother's sorority. She had been the president of the local chapter," Danielle said. "I have to represent my mom well. My entire life, I grew up with low self-esteem. The more I can achieve, the more I can feel better, temporarily. So I chased after achievement after achievement."

Her parents visited her at school shortly after her birthday in October of 2001 and pulled her out of classes for good. She received intensive treatment for months and transferred to Kent State University to be closer to home. Her life got back on track.

Severe depression returned a year later, and she was hospitalized multiple times. She spent the spring of 2004 recovering and worked closely with counselors and a psychiatrist. She graduated from Kent State with a degree in Journalism and Mass Communication that May.

There's so much shame surrounding depression. Her own grandmother said, "Don't tell anybody." But her mom set a new example. Danielle overheard her mom talking to one of her friends about it. Her mom told her, "Danielle, I don't know about you, but I need help with this. This is new to me. I need to get help."

Her mom set the example of getting help, of talking openly about it for healing. Danielle went to counseling and took medication.

"There's nothing wrong with medication. If you need it, take it," she said. "If you had heart issues or diabetes, you would take it. There's no shame in that."

After she graduated from college and started her first job, she made a pact with her church pastor and his wife, who is a licensed counselor. Danielle would do all the things it took to stay healthy. If they didn't work, she'd go back on the meds.

Would she be able to do her career? She kept praying and asked God, *What do you want?* She loved media too much to give up on it. She decided maybe she'd never be on TV, so she became a producer on the radio show I once hosted, The Regina Brett Show. It aired on WKSU, a National Public Radio affiliate in Kent, Ohio.

Still, the urge to be on TV tugged at her heart. For months she had been telling God, "If someone could have an open TV casting call, I'd go." She had no on-air experience but figured if she could just show them her personality, she could win them over.

Then one day her mom called to tell her a Cleveland TV station was holding an open casting call for a morning traffic reporter. It was the answer to her prayers. The station had people audition and asked viewers to vote. Danielle won. She beat out over 200 others. Her sorority sisters came out in full force and voted for her.

Those first broadcasts were bumpy.

"They asked for personality. I gave them it! It was the most unpolished traffic report you would ever hear," she said. "It set me apart."

People complained about how she pronounced words.

"It was horrible! It was absolutely horrible," she said, laughing. "Can I say that one more time? It was horrible! I left there every day crying. I knew how to write and tell stories, but traffic is all ad lib. All the strength I had and learned in journalism school was stripped away. All I had was my smile and the way that I dressed. I wasn't prepared for the backlash."

Viewers wrote nasty emails and Facebook comments: "She

sounds like she has tissues in her mouth . . . She is illiterate." Danielle was crushed.

"It's just different dialects people have. I needed more polish. It was tough. I didn't want to lose who I was but needed to speak in a way that everyone from every culture could understand me."

But her mom taught her not to quit, so she gave herself time. Today, she's a rising star on WKYC-TV where her smile lights up everyone's morning. Depression never completely left; she learned how to manage it so it doesn't control her or her life. She knows the support around her and within her is stronger than the lies depression will tell her.

"Some days are good, some are great, and others are really bad," she said. "However, I keep fighting. Depression is the thorn in my side that, like the apostle Paul in the Bible, I asked God to remove from me. However, my life shows that God's answer was the same to me as his answer to Paul: 'My grace is sufficient for you, for my power is perfected in weakness.'"

Recovery is a lifelong process.

"You live with it. I surround myself with people who know me and are supportive of me," she said. "I have a strong support system. My husband is my number one fan. He'll say, 'Go to sleep!' Sleep is important. I need to get rest, exercise to maintain my balance, be spiritually connected. My faith is important to me, to commune with God, to pray, to journal."

I'm so grateful Danielle shares her story. Too often we don't even know the people around us are suffering from depression. It's time we all removed the stigma, shame, and silence around mental health issues and talk about it, like Danielle. That way we can save lives.

The brain is a beautiful, complicated organ. We don't always understand how it works or why it doesn't. We need better research to understand how it works so we can better treat it when it doesn't work.

Until then, please remember this: Depression lies. Don't listen.

Instead, listen to everyone who loves you, and get help.

If you or someone you know is contemplating suicide, call the National Suicide Prevention Lifeline at 800-273-8255.

30

Pause to let peace in.

Ever catch yourself falling into that shame hole and trying to drag someone else with you? It doesn't happen as often as it used to, but it still happens to me.

One day, I was shopping at a local store where they started a self-service checkout option. I didn't want to use it, but the workers were encouraging people to try it. I set down my items—apparently in the wrong spot.

"Please place your item in bagging area," the computer ordered.

I moved them to the right.

"Please place your item in the bagging area," it repeated.

I moved them to the left. It refused to scan my items. Arrggh.

A cashier came over. "These didn't scan. None of them did," he said calmly and kindly.

What I heard was, "How stupid are you, lady?" Of course, he didn't say those words, but making a mistake sometimes pulls the trigger on my old childhood shame. The Buddhists call them *samskaras*, those past unpleasant experiences that get trapped inside us.

My frustration wasn't over him. It was over not knowing how to do something. I felt like the child I once was whose dad used to yell, "What the hell is wrong with you? Can't you do anything right?"

Only my dad has been dead since 1999, so it's really my voice saying it. I took over the job of shaming me, and sometimes shame comes out as anger.

I got snarky at the cashier, who was helpful and rang up my items for me.

"Next time I'll just shop somewhere else," I pouted.

Oh, what was I doing? What was I saying? I shoved my shame on him. I blamed some innocent, underpaid, kind worker. I felt like Fred Flintstone in that cartoon where an angel on one shoulder encourages him to do good while the devil on the other shoulder cheers on his bad behavior.

I'm sooo grateful no one videotaped my worst moment that day.

I left the store, but even as I walked out the door, I knew I had to come right back. My friends in recovery taught me that any time I'm emotionally disturbed by anything, no matter what the cause, the problem is me.

That means the solution is me.

They also taught me that when you're wrong, you promptly admit it.

So I got to my car, put in my items, dug in my wallet, and pulled out a five-dollar bill. I went back in and walked up to the cashier. He looked like a deer caught in the headlights of a semi truck.

"I was rude to you and I'm sorry," I said. "Here, thank you for helping me."

I handed him the tip, walked away, and hoped I didn't ruin any part of his day.

We've all had our moments when we are our worst selves.

It happens when someone says something rude or mean or criticizes you or your work or your parenting. Or life throws an inconvenience your way: a flat tire, a speeding ticket, a missed subway. Something doesn't turn out the way you had expected, and you lose your temper or your center of calm.

Sometimes it's a small thing: the copier breaks, you discover a stain on your shirt or a typo in your writing. But small things can provoke big feelings.

When my grandkids were little and got upset, my daughter told them: "It looks like you're having some big feelings about this." She tries not to judge them or take it personally if they cried or shouted or had a brief meltdown. She grew calmer, not louder, and acknowledged that big emotions are present.

My friends in recovery taught me how to handle big emotions. They use the *Twelve Steps and Twelve Traditions* book that says, "In all times of emotional disturbance or indecision, we can pause, ask for quiet, and in the stillness simply say: 'God grant me the serenity to accept the things I cannot change, courage to change the things I can, and the wisdom to know the difference. Thy will, not mine, be done.'"

They've taught me to pause before making decisions, to pray and get God on board, especially when I'm feeling stressed, overwhelmed or full of doubt.

Then there's the great teacher, Holocaust survivor Viktor Frankl. He had no power over what the Nazis did to him or his family in the Nazi concentration camps, but he had 100 percent control over his response. He taught us all that in between stimulus and response there's a gap, and in that gap, we have the power to choose our response, a mindful, intentional response.

In *Man's Search for Meaning,* the Holocaust survivor wrote, "Between stimulus and response there is a space. In that space is our power to choose our response. In our response lies our growth and our freedom."

To me, the key is to expand that space where I can challenge and change me. How? Here are some options:

The three-day wait:

Sometimes you can create a big buffer between you and what just happened. My friend Jill jokes about giving herself a three-day wait as a cooling-off period to respond to just about everything, especially family dramas.

Sometimes when you wait three days, you realize it's all none of your business and life simply sorts it out. Or those three days allow you to respond with grace, or to "cooperate with grace."

Gun safety advocates push for a mandatory three days between the time you buy a gun and when it is delivered. That way if someone wants to buy a gun in a fit of rage to hurt someone, by the time it arrives, the anger is gone.

When you buy a house, you get the closing documents three days before you close on the deal to give you time to understand all the terms and costs. It gives you time to absorb all that information before making such a big commitment.

In dating, many believe you should wait three days before you contact the person you just met. If you text or call too soon, you look too eager or needy. You can get their number and hit the pause button for three days. That way you aren't just acting on the "high" of just meeting. You can engage all of you—especially your brain—not just your emotions and hormones.

I've often used the three-day wait to make big purchases. If I'm spending more than 100 dollars on something and can wait, I will. Often, I decide not to buy it.

The two-minute warning:

The National Football League made the two-minute warning popular. The referees stop the game and inform both teams that there are only two minutes left on the clock. That way both teams can strategically plan their last plays of the game.

Many parents invoke the two-minute warning before it's time to stop playing and get ready for bed or school. My daughter will announce, "Two-minute warning!" when her three kids need to leave for soccer, take a shower, or leave for school. That way they can't claim, "I didn't know" or "You didn't tell me."

It works on me, too. I'll look at the clock and say, "Regina, you've got two more minutes to be on Facebook." It saves me from wasting a lot of time viewing cat videos I can live without.

The 90-second wait:

A minute and a half can feel like an eternity when your body has been hit by that rush of adrenaline that screams, "DO SOMETHING!" But that 90-second gap is precious time to take *not* reacting.

I love the book *Whole Brain Living* by Harvard brain scientist

Dr. Jill Bolte Taylor. She writes that it only takes 90 seconds to identify an emotion and allow it to dissipate. When you're scared or stressed, pause for 90 seconds, and let all that adrenaline find the exit ramp. It will once it finishes running through your body.

When something happens outside of you, there's a neurological process she calls the 90-second rule, a 90-second chemical process that happens. Chemicals flush through your body, putting it on full alert, like a car alarm blaring through your system. It takes about 90 seconds for that alarm to stop, for those stress chemicals to get flushed all the way out of your brain and your body.

We often hear about that "rush of adrenaline." It really does rush through your body, but only for about 90 seconds. Then it's gone.

What you do during those 90 seconds is important so that you don't stay caught in the loop of emotions that aren't helpful to you and others.

You don't focus on the problem or situation. You detach from it. You watch. You observe. You notice. You become curious.

You could set your phone timer for 90 seconds and watch the seconds tick down while you breathe as slowly and deeply as possible.

You could say a calming mantra, like, "All is well. All is well. All is well."

You could pray Psalm 23 or the Serenity Prayer or the Lord's Prayer or a round of Hail Marys.

You could be curious and ponder: *What is this moment asking of me?*

It's amazing how gently you can respond to life once you choose not to react to it.

One precious minute:

"I just need a minute."

I've often heard people say that. They just need a minute to wrap their head and heart around what was just said or what just happened.

Someone once said, "A minute is a moment with handles on it." I love that. You can grab onto it and hold on for dear life.

The day the nursing home called to say my mom had died, I drove there at 4:30 in the morning to be with her in spirit as they waited for paramedics to arrive to pronounce her dead. When I got to the door, a police officer stopped me.

"Ma'am, you can't go inside," he said, holding up his hand to stop me. "There's been a death."

I told him, "I know. My mom died." He still made me wait, as if it were a homicide investigation.

Instead of getting angry, I used that precious minute to pause, pray, and then proceed. I said the Serenity Prayer for my mom, for the staff inside who had found her, and for all ten of my siblings who had just lost their mother.

Once I got inside, there were no longer any big emotions. Just one.

Peace.

31

True love lasts for the long haul.

I did everything right.

I quarantined with an inner circle of family when the pandemic started. I socially distanced myself from everyone during the worst of the pandemic. I wore masks, so many and so often that I have a designated mask drawer.

I washed my hands so often that my skin got raw. I got vaccinated. Twice. Then I got the booster. And for two years, I was safe.

Then, out of the blue, when the infection rates were at a low, I got Covid.

Rats.

Who gave it to me? Who knows?

That morning I had taken the dog for a walk and felt fine. A few hours later, *Bam!* A horrible headache took over, then a sore throat and body aches. My entire body didn't feel right.

I took a home Covid test, swabbed both nostrils, swirled them in the tiny test tube liquid, and waited one minute. I stuck the paper stick in it for 10 minutes. When I pulled it out, a pink line appeared.

I took another one just to be sure. That pink line was even brighter.

Covid positive.

I told my husband, Bruce, then gathered up clothes for the week from our bedroom, all my bathroom needs (shampoo, conditioner, lotion, floss, toothbrush, deodorant, etc.), and my phone charger, and moved into the spare room upstairs.

I went online to reputable medical sites to find out what to do next: Quarantine for five days, mask up for five more. Stay home, stay away from him, hydrate, rest, take acetaminophen. Don't share a bedroom, bathroom, towels, or dishes. Wash your hands constantly and open windows for ventilation.

I built a little nest and surrounded myself with everything I needed to get well: Advil. Tylenol. Hand sanitizer. Water bottles. A humidifier. Tissues. Cough medicine. Cough drops.

All I did that day was sleep. Or try to. My throat and head hurt so bad they kept waking me up. Chills kept me tossing covers on and off.

The next day was our wedding anniversary. We were just getting back to going out to restaurants and gatherings after two years of being Covid careful. We had planned to go out for dinner at a nice restaurant and celebrate 26 years of wedded bliss. My husband usually jokes and trims off two years for cancer. He doesn't count those years as bliss, but I do.

Those two years were hard for both of us: the fear, the uncertainty, the challenges, the tests, the waiting, the procedures, the surgeries, the treatments, the loss of my hair, my breasts, my ovaries, my estrogen, my body as we knew and loved it. I wouldn't want to repeat those years, but they strengthened who we are alone and together.

Through every rough moment, Bruce would look at me, sometimes through tears, and remind me, "We're in this for the long haul."

Those simple words made me believe in a life after cancer. That cancer was just a speed bump on the highway of life. That we had a long, beautiful future ahead of us, and this was just a rough patch of potholes, a few bumps in the road, in a long road we would travel together for many more decades.

On our 26th wedding anniversary, we blew each other a kiss from across the room, both of us wearing masks. I thought of that beautiful summer day so long ago because this day was the same as our wedding day: clear, sunny with a bright blue sky.

When we married, I was 40; he was 42. The ages our kids are now. Back then, they were teenagers. Since he's Jewish and was divorced and I was raised Catholic, choosing a temple or church grew too complicated. Love is my religion and nature is my church, so we got married in a big park out in the country. We had an outdoor wedding with the sky as our cathedral. About 200 friends and family showed up. We had it catered with picnic food, barbecue style, so it felt like a family reunion.

That day we vowed to love and cherish each other through sickness and in health, in good times and in bad. We had no idea cancer would test those vows less than two years into our marriage.

We passed the test.

Covid was a mere pop quiz compared to cancer.

But it made me irritable. My entire back felt like one big pulled muscle. My face hurt from blowing my nose. My husband was loving, patient, and kind, even when I grew grumpy, whiny, and crabby.

My husband called my doctor. I grew up with a dad who didn't trust the world of medicine, so we usually just endured headaches, colds, and injuries. My husband grew up in a different world. You have an ache? You pop a pill. You have an injury? You see a doctor.

I felt so crappy I let him call. The doctor asked me a dozen questions. Since I was 66 years old, he prescribed the antiviral.

Bruce ran out and picked up the Paxlovid prescription. The aftertaste was awful. For hours, your mouth tastes like you licked rust off the bottom of a car. It reminded me of the chemo drugs. Those, too, came with many pages of side effects, including death. I was so afraid to take chemo, but my husband reminded me, if you read the side effects on aspirin, you wouldn't take that either.

Bruce ran to the store to buy things to kill the bad taste. He came back with a huge bag of gum, cough drops, Tic Tacs, and Altoids. He also brought something to surprise me.

"I brought us a treat to celebrate," he said.

We talked about our wedding day, that June 22, 1996. We shook our heads about how I was diagnosed with breast cancer two years into our marriage, in February 1998. On this, our 26th anniversary, we didn't renew our vows, but we renewed our mantra: "We're in this for the long haul."

Then my hubby brought out two luscious custard tarts brimming with raspberries, blackberries, and strawberries. And our favorite dessert: chocolate coconut bars. How decadent. We ate the desserts standing eight feet apart, laughing about not being able to even exchange a kiss or hold hands.

All week he did what love does. All those small actions. He did the dishes. He fixed me food. He walked the dog. He ran to the store every single time I needed something. And he never complained.

He was, and is, my cheerleader, my coach, my partner through the best and worst of times.

When I'm sick, he reminds me: Don't believe anything you think. When I'm sick, boredom and restlessness set in. I start contemplating the cosmos and questioning everything in my life. Now is not the time to make any major decisions, he tells me. You are under the influence of illness. When I'm sick, my mind drifts into places that I shouldn't go.

Bruce saves me during those times. Somehow he can find me before I get too lost.

Bruce is my guardrail. He keeps me centered on the highway of life, keeps me from flying solo and spinning out of control.

Sometimes we're flying over the speed limit, sometimes we're stuck in the slow lane of life, but we're together, always, for the long haul.

32

There's always Plan Be.

It's usually the first thing we ask someone we meet: What do you do?

The question sometimes feels like an indictment. It's asked at every party, on every first date, and at every momentary meeting. That question is the doorway to explore who you are. But are you really what you do?

You start to answer, and it feels like you're flailing to grab a rung on the ladder of life's worth.

I've been at schmoozing events and watched high-powered corporate types skip right over the spouses because that's what they see them as, mere spouses, not women or men with their own interesting identities, worth, and value.

I've been in conversations where the person allegedly conversing is scanning the room looking for someone more important to talk to. They don't even bother to make eye contact with you, they're just a bobblehead bouncing up and down and back and forth as they see who else is on the radar screen to impress.

What do you do?

That's often the first question we ask or are asked at social events. An article in the *Wall Street Journal* by Rachel Feintzeig challenged people to move past the work question, which too often feels like the "worth" question.

You hear it at dinner parties, temple, and church events, any time you venture out of your inner circle: "So what do you do?"

I'm sometimes tempted to answer, "Anything I want."

Or, "It's Top Secret. If I told you, I'd have to kill you."

Okay, so I've been watching too many spy thrillers.

Our doing is often our undoing. We're often too busy, too overscheduled, and too tied to our work world to have a life full of joy and mystery and stories to tell.

Feintzeig wrote in her article, "Some of us grasp onto our titles like a life raft, convinced they're the thing that makes us worth talking to. Others blurt out the query because it's easy, acceptable small talk—or because we have let our jobs eat up so much of our time we have no room for anything else.

"What would happen if we didn't lead with our professional selves?"

No, you won't drown. You don't need that life raft. You need a life.

A few weeks ago, a good friend called to say goodbye to my husband. His friend Richard called to say he was dying. He wanted to say farewell to a good friend. What an honor, to be chosen for that last call.

That call jolted me awake. The friend had been a work colleague at the top of his game for so long, I couldn't imagine him ever quitting. Cancer will do that. Knock the doing right out of you.

Retirement knocks the rungs out from under you, too. Who

are you now? Maybe anything you want to be. As the saying goes, It's never too late to be the person you were meant to be. Go exploring and find out. You don't have to lead with who you used to be.

We're all a lot of things. I'm a columnist and a grandmother of three. I'm an author and a woman who loves to kayak, hike, shoot archery, and attempt to line dance to '90s country music.

Instead of asking people, What do you do? What if we all expand our questions:

What's your passion? What do you enjoy doing most? Oops, there's that DOing again. What hobbies do you enjoy? Do you have any pets? Where did your parents or grandparents come from? What are you reading? What shows are you watching? Where did you grow up? What's your favorite way to spend time?

What trips have you taken? What trips do you want to take? Tell me a story about your goldendoodle or grandson or gramma that made you laugh out loud.

What brings you joy? That question has led to some deep conversations with people who look at me stunned and say, I have no idea. They confide that they haven't experienced joy in a while, then we launch into a deep discussion about how to change that.

What's your superpower? My husband can identify people by the back of their heads. When he's behind someone, he instantly knows who is walking in front of him. I can barely remember their name even if I had lunch with them last month.

My superpower? Getting people unstuck. If you lead with, "I can't . . ." or "I don't know how to . . ." you'll leave with five steps you can take to change that.

What do you do for fun? It doesn't have to be skydiving, deep sea diving, or white-water rafting. My fun? Coaching archery, playing hide and seek with the grandkids, and playing card games with my daughter.

Instead of focusing on your resume lives, it's time to live the kind of life you want people to remember and celebrate long after you're gone.

You are more than what you do.

So is everyone else.

33

The best friends show you how to be a better friend.

One day death will crack the inner circle.

One day you'll look around the table at Christmas, Easter, or Passover, and that one dear friend you could always count on to add more joy and food and meaning to the occasion won't be there to celebrate any more.

When my friend Ed's big, beautiful heart gave out, it broke the hearts of all who loved him. Ed Rafferty was a pillar in the recovery community, one we never expected to fall.

His obituary listed his occupation as a heavy equipment operator for the city of Ravenna. That's just what he did to pay the rent. That wasn't his mission in life.

His mission in life was to save lives. In his 43 years of sobriety, he saved countless lives, including mine. His mission was to help alcoholics and addicts who wanted a new way of life. Ed was the doorway to the new life. If there really is a Book of Life, Ed helped people turn the page to start a new chapter, to write a new beginning, and to create a happily ever after for their families.

He always called me sweetie and served as my guardian

angel, protecting me from myself when I was in my late 20s and attracted to men who didn't respect me. Ed, who was faithfully married, was the big brother who knew I deserved better before I did.

As the decades of our friendship evolved, every time I asked, "Ed, how are you?" he answered, "I'm old." He wasn't putting himself down. He believed aging was just another word for living, and he was grateful for every day sobriety gave him.

After he died at age 75, I read all his Facebook posts and laughed so hard, I cried harder than I had cried over losing him.

Gems like:

"I walk around like everything is fine, but deep down, inside my shoe, my sock is falling off . . . People are so judgmental; I can tell by looking at them . . . If you wait long enough to cook breakfast, everyone will eat cereal. Follow me for more cooking tips."

Ed's dad died young, in his 50s, from heart disease. Ed knew his days, too, might be numbered because of bad genetics. After his first heart incident, Ed changed his entire life. He became a vegan and lost weight. He took up meditation and even did a retreat with the Buddhist monk Thich Nhat Hanh.

Ed was serious when it mattered most and the king of corny jokes the rest of the time. He loved making people laugh with these quotes:

"The divorce rate among my socks is astonishing . . . I don't always roll a joint. But when I do, it's my ankle . . . I hate it when people try to act all intelligent and talk about Mozart when they have never even seen one of his paintings . . . Time to get up and get going. Today's bad decisions aren't going to make themselves."

He also posted serious sayings: "You were born an original, don't die a copy . . . You don't always have to tell your side of the story. Time will."

There was so much recovery tucked into the wisdom he quoted: "Trying to hurt me by bringing up my past is like trying to rob my old house. I don't live there anymore . . . Be the type of person that leaves a mark, not a scar . . . Heal so you don't hurt people who didn't hurt you."

He jokingly referred to his wife as "my higher power." He loved calling her "My Melanie" and his daughter "My Amy." He didn't just love them; he cherished them.

Sobriety gave him so many gifts he wanted us all to have: "Addiction is when you give up everything for one thing. Recovery is when you give up one thing for everything." Or as someone else said, "You can have a drink or everything else."

Ed gained everything when he quit drinking: the love of his wife, his children, his grandchildren, and countless friends.

Aging didn't bother him. He knew it was a gift denied many. "If you think that life is too short, do something about it."

Ed did something about it. He extended his life as long as he could, but it was still too short for all of us who loved him.

Then there was my friend, Jim. By the time we learned that Jim had brain cancer, our dear friend was heading to hospice.

Jim Samuels wasn't just our friend. He was everybody's friend.

His Super Bowl parties were legendary. He was one of the few friends my husband had who truly cared about sports. My husband didn't get a sports gene, but he was great at making friends and brought Jim into my life.

I'm not sure Jim actually loved sports; he just loved bringing people together. He was a great connector until the day he died at 68.

Some people collect coins or stamps or baseball cards. Jim collected people. I am so fortunate to have been one of them. He kept every friend he ever made. My dear friend Cheryl Davis, who was one of Jim's closest friends, said, "If you can only have one friend, pick Jim."

We were lucky he picked us.

Every friend Jim made became a lifelong friend. He was so easy to love, and he made it seem like you were easy to love, even those of us who aren't, like me. I have a lot of rough edges, but Jim never cared. He didn't care if I showed up to his parties late or empty-handed or hogged all the guacamole. He always greeted me with open arms and the biggest smile.

Jim made you want to be a better person. He was the guy who never missed a funeral, who always took your call, who rarely said an unkind word about anyone, even people everyone else talked about.

I'm not always the best friend. Jim helped me become a better one. He showed me how. I watched how he greeted every single person like they were the most important person in the room, whether it was his living room, board room, or conference room. Because to Jim, they were. Everyone was important to him.

I sometimes make plans, then cancel at the last minute. I add too much to the calendar. I try to wedge my friends into an overflowing life. My friends love me anyway. They say friends are the family your heart gets to choose. Jim chose me in spite of all my flaws.

Every winter, a hundred of us trudged through the snow to

his home in a Cleveland suburb where he had stacks of pizza, tables of decadent desserts, and the biggest TV screen ever created.

One summer he went with us on vacation for a week. The Outer Banks of North Carolina offered sun, sand, and endless sea. Jim wanted more. He didn't know what to do with himself. Jim suffered from FOMO. Fear of Missing Out. He had one setting: ON. And because of that, he wanted to be everywhere, everywhere the action was. There wasn't much action on the beach unless you count the sand pipers, sea gulls, and surfers.

How fitting that we got the news that he died the morning we left for our annual vacation. My husband and I talked about Jim during the 11-hour drive. Later that week, we sat in our hotel room and watched his funeral streaming live.

The eulogies called him decent, loyal, kind. They said he was the first to arrive, the last to leave, and the one who made everyone feel like they truly mattered. They talked about his love for his faith, his family, his friends.

They joked about how we used to call Jim a "serial dater." He dated just about every woman in Cleveland and magically stayed friends with them all. I never heard any of the women say a bad word about him. Only that he was "too nice."

He was that big teddy bear of a guy, with beady brown eyes, glasses, and a comb-over of brown hair that didn't stand a chance of covering that big head of his.

Jim found the perfect life partner when he found Ofelia, who "cracked the Jim code," as someone said at his funeral. She grounded him, steadied him, and supported him always, all the way until he died.

Jim was goofy, but we loved that about him. Part of him was

still 10 years old inside. He'd call his nephew Hank "Hanky." He'd leave a phone message saying it was "Slim Jamuels" calling. He was so corny that sometimes even he would groan at what came out of his mouth.

He would instantly switch to Mr. Serious when it came to his work as senior vice president at Guggenheim Commercial Real Estate or his love for Israel. Jim dedicated his life to *tikkun olam,* to making the world whole. He was like a kid plugging holes in a leaky dam; he had his fingers in everything, trying to make a difference, trying to stop someone else's pain.

His sister, Arlene, called him a "one of a kind, a friend to everybody . . . He had a lot of friends, but everyone thought of him as their best friend. He was my brother. When you talk about family, he was every sense of family. Always there for us, no matter what."

And even though he never married, he was a great matchmaker. He set up 13 couples and probably kept another dozen together by lending an ear to listen to their woes.

I found out he was co-chair of his high school reunion for 40 years. Yes, he was THAT guy. The one everyone loved. The one everyone could count on.

That's why his temple created the James A. Samuels Social Action Fund. Those are two perfect words to describe Jim: Social and action.

Rest in peace? Not a chance. Not Jim.

Even as he lay dying, his room was a confetti mess of sticky notes and cards. The constant stream of visitors led one nurse to ask, "Who is this man? A celebrity?"

Yes, Jim Samuels was a celebrity.

He was our VIP, famous for putting everyone else first.

34

Every day answer the call to create.

Every day there are a million reasons not to write.

It's raining. It's snowing. It's too beautiful outside to be stuck at a computer all day long.

My siblings will hate me. My parents will haunt me. My readers will hassle me over some sentence they didn't like.

The last book I wrote didn't get published. I made a typo in my blog, and someone rubbed my nose in it. I don't feel inspired today.

There are endless reasons not to write.

Write anyway.

Many years ago I made a vow to God. I was feeling all kinds of disturbance within, the fear and doubt swirled around in me like an inner tornado. It was a gorgeous winter night, and snow was tumbling out of the sky. Not falling, but tumbling down in huge clumps, like the angels above made me the target of their snowball fight to get my attention, and man, did they have good aim.

I looked up into all that white and said, "Yes. Yes! I will be your writer. I will write whatever You want me to write." Then I wept. Not out of joy, but out of pure surrender to God's will, no matter what it might mean.

Many of us ignore the call to create. It might take the form of cooking, gardening, carpentry, singing, painting, or photography. It takes a toll on your soul to say yes and do it, but it takes a greater toll on your soul not to do it, to say no.

The reason I said a resounding "Yes!" to God that night was because for years I had said a meager, weak "Yes!" but took no action to back it up. I only wrote in diaries where my words were safe and secret from the world. Then one night after my evening prayer, it hit me: What if God gives up on me and asks someone else? What if God simply takes the gift back because I'm not using it? That scared me more than using it.

So I said yes and I keep saying yes.

My friend Karen Sandstrom says yes every day. She creates something every single day. I get a slice of joy every morning when I go on Facebook and see her #tinymorningsketch. It's like being on a magic carpet ride that takes you back to being five, six, or seven years old, when the entire world was a wonderland and still is.

Her characters emerge from her imagination that she releases from her daily drawing practice. There's an elephant picking sparkle berries. A banjo-playing bear. A dog named Henry, whose BFF is a little girl named Hope who notices and celebrates the beauty in every moment.

Karen was once a book editor at the *Plain Dealer* where I was a columnist. Now she illustrates children's books. Her advice?

"Get your butt in the chair and do the work. You make room for material to emerge when you do that," she said. "I

draw every day or virtually every day. Sometimes the characters come out of a wish to create a character, sometimes they
come out of a wish to create a mood or make a statement with
drawing. It just depends. But they come because I invite them
in through sitting down with a pencil."

When she's not writing or drawing, restlessness nags at her
soul.

"I call it the wolf at the door," Karen said. "The only way
to keep that wolf away from your door is to write. It doesn't
matter, just do it. You're going to feel bad until the moment you
sit down and focus on the work."

"I get up early in the morning so I have time to do the thing
I love, which is drawing, before any other claims are made on
my day," she said. "Whatever it is, the thing that you love to do,
if you can get up early and get it done, the rest of the day will
feel better. You will be a more whole person because you've
taken care of the thing you most love to do."

Take care of the thing you most love to do. Make it an act
of love. That's what novelist Paula McLain does.

I had the joy and honor of interviewing *New York Times* best-
selling author Paula McLain to launch the paperback version of
her book *When the Stars Go Dark*. It was an online event with
Book Passage supported by six bookstores.

Like Ernest Hemingway, Paula keeps track of her word
count every day in a little notebook.

"It helps me feel I am tied to an endeavor that has a certain
level of integrity," she said. "Like, I've made a promise to these
pages, a promise to these words. That helps me work."

She aims to write 1,000 words a day, every day, even on weekends.

"On a good day I do that," she said. "I just put my ass in the chair, then I write it down on little pieces of paper and I put them in a box, a manuscript box with all the pages that I've written. It seems sacred in a way."

It does. Saying "Yes" is sacred. Following through on that yes blesses others, making it even more sacred.

"You say yes," she said. "That's exactly the process you use as a writer. You say yes to the unknown. You say yes to uncertainty. You say yes to the subconscious. You say yes to the story that hasn't been written yet. You just surrender."

Every. Single. Day.

That's real commitment.

"It's commitment, but it feels like devotion," she said.

Oooh. Devotion sounds so much better.

"It's out of love," she said. "I say often to young writers, just touch it every day. Open your file and touch it every day. Have a conversation with it and see what happens."

I love the idea of calling creating devotional. It feels holy, not like a burden, but an invitation from God, the Universe, the Great Muse. Paula even lights a candle when she writes.

Devotion sounds so much better than calling it discipline. Too many people say it takes discipline to write. Having been abused as a child in the name of discipline, I don't want anything to do with that word. But devotion, that sounds like something I want.

"The ruler doesn't work for me either," Paula said. "This is where I bring my softest, highest self."

What a great description of our best self. That's the person I want writing: my softest, highest self. Not my fearful, doubting self.

I meet so many people who want to be writers, but calling it "discipline" scares them away from the keyboard. When you call it devotional, that sounds like an invitation to something you want to experience. Your desk becomes an altar, a place where you meet God and co-create with the Creator of all.

"We all want devotion, we all want love, not fear," Paula said.

After our interview, a box arrived in the mail. It was a thank-you gift from Paula. I opened it up and found gifts tucked in a nest of confetti paper: a small jar of honey, a packet of black tea, a shiny tea ball steeper, and a guava honey essential-oil candle. She ordered it from Thistle Farms, a sanctuary of hope for women in Nashville, Tennessee, who survived addiction, trafficking, and prostitution. The card inside said, "Love is the most powerful force for change in the world."

The words on the candle? "Love Heals."

That's what the best writing does. It heals.

That candle transformed my writing desk into an altar.

When you create, it creates a path, an escape hatch, an exit ramp for other people's grief or sadness or fear or pain to be released. When you see writing, or any creating, as an act of love, it blesses the reader, the viewer, the receiver in ways you will never know.

That's why Paula writes no matter how she feels.

"Whatever inspiration is," she said, "it's mercurial and it's magical and we do not have any control over it."

Or any control over how it will bless the world.

"Instead of going to the mall and shoe shopping, I'm going to sit down and I'm going to light my candle and say, 'I'm show-ing up there. I'm going to write my words, and whether or not they change the fate of fiction, they are evidence that I was here.'"

Give the world evidence you were here.

Sit down, say yes, and devote yourself to healing the world.

35

Play harder than you work.

My dad gave all 11 of his kids a great work ethic. What he didn't give us was a play ethic.

My dad's entire life was work. Hard work. The kind that stains and scars your hands. The kind that hurts your back and strains your muscles. The kind that leaves you exhausted at the end of every day.

Some men shower before work; then there are those who shower after work, who rinse off a day of sweat and grime. Blue collar guys like my dad.

His younger sister Kate once told me that my dad never had a childhood. He was the oldest boy in a family of ten children. His parents, Irish immigrants, survived the poverty of Ireland, only to suffer the poverty of America.

When the Great Depression hit, they lost their home, their farm, and a whole way of life they could count on for food, clothing, and shelter. My dad, who was 14, had put in the corn crop, so the auctioneer said he should get the 600 dollars. Tom Brett used it to help purchase a shack on the railroad tracks in a nearby small town called Ravenna.

He transformed that dump into a home for his younger siblings. That became my one and only childhood home.

We Bretts have a strong work ethic. What we don't know how to do is stop. I'm just now exploring what it means to have a strong play ethic, not just to play on weekends and vacations, but to play every day of the week, to have a joy agenda.

The most fun I ever had at work was as a journalist for the *Akron Beacon Journal.* Don't get me wrong, we committed serious journalism there. The paper won two Pulitzer Prizes during the time I was there, and we still had a lot more fun than any employees have the right to.

One colleague brought in a giant blow-up dinosaur that hung like a Macy's Parade balloon over our business desk. We all decorated our work areas with wind-up toys, signs, and posters. One editor kept a candy jar filled on her desk that we emptied weekly.

We held cake bake-offs and chili contests and had tailgate parties on the parking deck. There was usually a euchre game going on in the lunchroom or a walking club heading out at lunchtime.

We worked hard, but we played hard, too. It made us a stronger team.

My friend Beth once asked, "What if, at the end of your life, you had to account for all the fun you missed? For all the joy you set aside?"

Yikes. Most of us would be guilty of being way too boring.

People often ask, "Are we having fun yet?" in a sarcastic tone when they're stuck doing something boring or tedious. But it's a question to seriously ask yourself.

Are you having fun?

I think fun is highly underrated. Work seems to be the driving force, not joy. Not for my buddy Hal.

Way back in 1982, Hal Becker was diagnosed with terminal cancer. They gave him three months to live. He was just 28 years old.

Instead of killing him, cancer made him eternally grateful. He made a vow to have fun and has kept that vow ever since. He's now in his 60s and truly is one of the most joyful people I know, even after he was diagnosed with cancer again in his 60s.

I call him Mister Happy. He absolutely insists on enjoying life.

For years he was a nationally known expert on sales, customer service, and negotiating. He conducted seminars and assisted clients like IBM, Disney, New York Life, United Airlines, Verizon, and AT&T.

At age 22, Hal was Xerox's Number One salesperson among a national sales force of 11,000. Then Hal founded and became CEO of Direct Opinions, one of America's first customer service telemarketing firms that administered more than two million calls per year.

For years he lectured around the world. He received the Toastmasters International Communication and Leadership Award, one of only eight people in the world to be given this honor.

His dad, Joe, was a bookie. He used to tell stories about Cleveland's betting scene. Joe made a ton of money, but he went straight when Hal was born and became a used-car dealer. He called them clunkers.

They rented a two-family home. He watched his dad when someone returned a car.

"Want your money back? Take whatever car you want on the lot," his dad would tell the customer. They called him "Honest Joe." Hal would say, "Pop, the guy picked out a more expensive car."

"So? He'll come back," his dad said. "Trust me."

An only child, Hal calls his parents his heroes. They gave him love until they both died when he was in his 30s.

When Hal was diagnosed with stage III testicular cancer, it had already spread to his abdomen, chest, and brain.

"I remember feeling sick, like I had been kicked in the stomach," he said. It was Christmas Eve when the pain hit, but it wasn't until February that he went to the doctor. They gave him three months to live.

Treatment options were experimental at the time. He vowed to beat it and did. His parents and friends stayed by his side through it all. It was the first time he had seen his father cry. I carry a picture of myself bald from chemo; he carries a photo of himself at 83 pounds with burn marks on his arms from the chemotherapy.

Hal doesn't go a day without joy. Even at work. Especially at work.

Instead of killing him, cancer made him eternally grateful. Even after he got cancer again decades later.

Hal made a vow to have fun back in 1982, and he has kept it every day since. He wrote four business books, including the witty, *Can I Have 5 Minutes of Your Time?* He's a drummer in a band, plays golf, and flies an ultralight plane. He traveled often for work and saved hundreds of bottles of free hotel shampoo, conditioner, and lotion and donated them to the women's shelters in Cleveland.

He makes it all a joy. He works hard, but he plays harder.

Hal is like an eternal 10-year-old. Like a puppy that never grew up. His energy and enthusiasm for life is contagious.

"I just get up every day, and say, *Wow*. It's another day. I love getting up and making myself happy," he told me.

"We all have to do stuff we don't want to do, but I'll try to add a spin to it, then get it over with so we can get to something fun.

"You have to love what you do for your job," he tells everyone. He shared "Hal's Twinkie Rules" with me:

Be like a kid; don't lose that fun inside of you. Trust me, it is more fun to be around fun people, not people who are serious all the time.

At work, pretend you're playing. You will see that you and your employees do a better job and enjoy it more. Look at the ticket counters at the airport, then go to the Southwest ticket counter. They are having more fun.

Learn from Disney. They are just an amusement park, but they do it better than anyone else, and they enjoy beating the competition.

Your attitude is everything. If you want to have fun, you will. Remember, you have to eat a lot of cereal to find the free toy.

Don't lose touch with the child inside of you.

If you're married, be a great spouse. If you're a parent, be a great parent. If you want great friends, be a great friend.

You can be anything you want to be when you grow up. Are you really doing what you want to do with your life? If not, then when will you make yourself happy?

Start today. Get out and play.

36

Contemplating death can turbocharge your life.

Death is the ultimate spiritual adventure, the one nobody wants to take. Yet the only guarantee in life is that it ends.

That's the cold, hard truth. We are all going to die. Death has my name. Yours, too. That isn't a threat. It's a promise. One that will come true for every single one of us.

The mystery is when.

You have two dates on a tombstone: the day you enter life, and the day you enter eternal life. What you do with the dash in the middle is all up to you.

I've heard that if you meditate on death daily, it will change how you live every single day.

My brother Matt once told me about an app called WeCroak, so I bought it for 99 cents. Croak is another euphemism for death, like kick the bucket. WeCroak reminds you five times a day that you're going to die. That's all it does.

Co-founder New York publicist Hansa Bergwall described it this way: "It's a passion project and mindfulness tool that's hit a chord around the world because of death's power to ground us in what's real." He and Ian Thomas, an app creator, launched WeCroak in 2017.

It encourages you to "wake up to the truth about death, live immediately, enjoy life more and find ways to hone our habits and ourselves."

A Bhutanese saying inspired their movement: "To be a happy person, one must contemplate death five times daily." I respect the Bhutanese, so five times a day, my screen goes black, and white words show up to tell me, "Don't forget, you are going to die."

It's not as morbid as you think, but then again, I once picked up bodies for a funeral home to pay the rent, so my version of morbid might not match yours.

The WeCroak website says: "Our invitations come at random times and at any moment, just like death." Open the app and you find a quote about death from a poet, philosopher, or famous person. Then you're supposed to take a moment to contemplate, breathe, meditate on your mortality, then let go of what doesn't matter and honor what does.

That's it. No bios on the quote writer. No ads. No links. It does just one thing: remind you that you are going to die. The point is to get the reminder, then get off your phone and sink deeper into the present moment, not into Facebook or Twitter or TikTok.

It's kind of like actor Robin Williams whispering in your ear, "Carpe diem!" The fact that Williams is gone makes those Latin words "seize the day" even more powerful.

Some of the quotes are on the mystical side: "Many have died; you also will die. The drum of death is being beaten. The world has fallen in love with a dream. Only the sayings of the wise will remain."—Kabir

Or blunt, like Chinese philosopher Lao Tzu: "People are born soft and weak. They die hard and stiff."

Or gentle: "Death is the sound of distant thunder at a picnic"—W. H. Auden.

Gloomy. Uplifting. Irreverent. Death is all that and more. No matter the mood, each quote is a good reminder to put your phone down and live the life that's right in front of you.

Death is a story we tell ourselves. What story do you tell yourself about it? Some people believe the deceased goes to heaven or hell or to purgatory to pay off their sins. Others see it as a flight we can't go on. I've heard death called "a change of address."

I don't believe people die by accident, injury, or mistakes. I believe they complete their lives here. That's the story I tell myself about death. It's not an ending. It's a completion of a person's soul journey.

For years I worked in a funeral home. I went on death calls in the middle of the night to peoples' homes, to nursing homes, and to hospitals. I also worked as an emergency medical technician on an ambulance. Some people died even though I did my best to save them.

I used to feel I failed them, like the little boy who hanged himself accidentally on a rope, the one I gave my breath to on that long ambulance drive to the hospital. Or the man with kidney failure we were unable to save, or the man whose heart gave out as soon as we reached the emergency room.

I've witnessed numerous deaths. When my husband's father

died, we stood vigil around his bed as he took his last breath. When my friend's daughter overdosed and her brain no longer functioned, we gathered around her bed in the Intensive Care Unit at the hospital to help her let go. We prayed and sang her Home.

When my Uncle Paul was sick with cancer, two sisters came to visit me, and we drove an hour to visit him. When we arrived, one sister, who is a nurse, realized he was in the process of dying. He was slipping gently away, so we gathered around his bed, prayed, and told him his beautiful bride was waiting for him there.

My spiritual guide Lynn tells me people die when they're ready. They leave when they're bored, bitter, or have completed their lives. She once told me my soul had three exit options.

When she told me that, she said I had already declined one exit. Was it the year I had cancer? She said, no, it had been the year she encouraged me to take THE best care of my body.

I had been overly busy and neglecting sleep. One day my mind was so busy, I drove right through a red traffic light without stopping. I was so grateful no one else was in the intersection.

That year when I spoke to her, she told me to be vigilant about my health. She told me to "check in" with myself hourly. Was I hungry? Thirsty? Tired? All year, I was extra good to my body. At the end of the year, when I asked her about my health, she said, "Well, you're still here."

Whew. I made it!

She told me I had another "exit" window in my mid-60s. So when I hit 64, I asked her what I needed to do to stick around and grow even older.

"Actively participate in your life," she said. Get involved. Find adventures every day. Let life know you want to stay.

So I got busy living. I spent more time hiking and kayaking. I got a dog. I tried to snow ski, Rollerblade, and took speed-skating lessons, which ended in a fall that gave me a slight concussion, but, hey, I was busy participating in life.

That year, a terrible storm hit as I was driving home. A block from my house, I stopped at a traffic light as the wind roared around me. Suddenly, I heard a loud *crack!* A giant tree just eight feet from my car cracked in half and fell. Thankfully, it missed my car. I looked up, and the traffic light was no longer above me. It had crashed ten feet in front of my car.

That's when I knew it. I had cleared the second "exit." Whew! If Lynn is right, I'll live at least into my late 80s.

I don't need a lot of help contemplating death. The funeral home job put me face-to-face with death. And surviving breast cancer gave me a great gift: I wake up every day with scars on my chest where my breasts used to be. They remind me to live the hell out of this day.

Remembering we all die can turbocharge your living.

One day I was exhausted after hosting the three grandkids for a sleepover, going to two of their soccer games, playing dolls and Chinese checkers, and losing to Scrabble when their parents invited me to drive an hour away to go a hot air balloon festival at sunset. More fun with the kids, or go home and relax in front of the TV?

Bring on the fun!

So I squeezed into the way back of their van, tucked my knees into the seat in front of me, talked to Asher, age 10, about the Cleveland baseball team's wild card options, held hands

with River, 6 and giggled with Ainsley, 8. We saw hot air bal-
loons soar, ate funnel cakes, and raced around under the stars. I
got to lift my grandson into a giant tree to climb, piggyback the
youngest back to the van, and tuck my jacket under the head
of her sleepy sister on the ride home.

That night I slept the sleep of the dead and smiled when I
woke to another reminder: "Don't forget, you're going to die."

I'm good with that.

37

Live your eulogy now.

Every morning, life confronts us with choices: Eat the doughnut or the bagel? Take the subway or the taxi? Wear the red tie or the blue one? Feed the kids cereal or toast?

Sometimes those questions distract us from the deeper questions that really matter. Like the question in my medicine cabinet that challenges me every morning and keeps me awake some nights:

"If today were the last day of my life, would I want to do what I'm about to do today?"

The words belong to Steve Jobs, the Apple founder who shared them with Stanford University graduates after he had been diagnosed with the cancer that eventually killed him.

Arianna Huffington framed the question a different way: "Are you living your eulogy or your resume?"

She was inspired by President Barack Obama after he eulogized the men and women who died in the Washington Navy Yard shooting. Obama shared how the victims gave dictionaries to third graders, ran the children's Bible study at church, and loved their children and grandkids.

Huffington questioned in her blog post why eulogies celebrate life so differently from "the way we define success in our everyday existence."

It has taken years for me to get a better balance, to consciously choose eulogy living over resume building.

For a long time, I defined myself by my writing successes. In the news business, when a journalist wins a Pulitzer Prize, they tell the winner, "That will be the first line in your obituary."

Sadly, they're probably right. But is the biggest award you win in life the thing that defines you the most? I hope not.

I think it's sad that grandkids show up at the end of obituaries, way behind the list of work achievements, social clubs, and survivors. Why last? If you've got grandkids, you know they're first when it comes to the joy in your life. At least mine are.

Some people hate funerals. I find them inspiring. They remind us that every life has an end, that now is the time to deepen our dash—that place on the tombstone between our birth and our death.

How do you want to fill in the gap between the person you are today and the person you want to be?

I've never forgotten the story one woman shared with me about a funeral she attended, where a child, age nine, gave a brief eulogy for her grandma. The child surprised them all when she said, "Grandma wore red lipstick and drove with the top down." What a way to live. Bright, bold, and beautiful.

I want my grandkids to speak at my funeral. They see me through eyes of love, joy, and wonder.

When little River was four, she found the plastic eggs in the basement that I fill with candy for the annual Easter egg hunt. Instead of ruining the Easter Bunny's identity, it was a magic discovery. She told the kids at her preschool that I was the Easter Bunny's helper.

Uh oh, I thought, would they now stop believing?

No. They said to her, "I wish *my* gramma was the Easter Bunny's assistant." I love that's how she sees me.

How do people see you?

When it comes to living your eulogy, write it out before someone else does after you're gone. The only time to change it is now.

Sit down, close your eyes, and imagine your own funeral. Try it. Who will be there? And who won't? The son you stopped speaking to? The brother you cut out of your life and can't remember why? There's still time to heal those relationships.

Who will speak on your behalf? Your spouse, kids, friends, coworkers, or siblings? What will they say? Write it all down: Your personality traits. Passions. Funny quirks. Sayings. Your goals, legacy, and lessons. What you created or contributed to improve the world.

First, write the truth of what you think they will say. Then get quiet, and in silence and solitude, write down how you *want* to be remembered. Write a eulogy worth living. How well does that eulogy match the life you are currently living?

Now is the time to realign your life. Have your eulogy match your life.

What will yours say?

For the longest time, I spent my life building my resume. Those writing awards that once mattered so much to me are now in a landfill. When we moved two years ago, I gathered them all, savored them one last time, and said goodbye. I didn't want my kids or grandkids fretting over what to do with them.

I want my life of loving them to matter to them, not my career.

I want my grandson to remember the day I was throwing him the football and his friend said, "Man, your grandma has an arm on her." I do throw a wicked spiral and can kick that ball higher than his house.

I hope my granddaughter sews with her children the way we did, making pillows for all her fifth-grade teachers. She ran the sewing machine; I stuffed the pillows.

I want the youngest to pass along her love of board games and let her kids beat her, like I do pretty much every time we play.

I want them to remember me for saying yes to fun, to that epic snowball fight we had one night at 10 p.m., and for getting them a puppy they get to love and I get to clean up after.

My friend Barbie is no stranger to death. She married at 20 and became a widow at 39. She once posted this question on Facebook: "What stories would you tell at my funeral?"

What stories will they tell at yours?

She wanted to hear some of them while she was still alive. Friends wrote:

"When you meet Barbie for the first time, she makes you feel like you have known each other your whole lives."

"This girl would do snow angels in her bikini." Which she does every first snowfall.

"How about a 60-mph ride thru the mountains in a van with a hundred stuffed animals on the dashboard and a windshield that needed to be cleaned a year ago."

"She was a master of living every day to the fullest. She loved the world and the people in it. Empowering and loving people were her love language."

The lives we're living now, that's what will make up the stories people will not only tell about you but remember for the rest of their lives.

Give them good material.

38

Make a beautiful mess of your life.

Make your bed. Wear sunscreen. Dance like no one is watching.

Every year people offer graduation advice to inspire the next generation.

March to the beat of your own drummer. Stay hungry, stay foolish. In a world where you can be anything, be kind.

Every spring, thousands of graduates are forced to listen to profound graduation advice from people who think they know something that will give them a rocket boost to start their new lives.

Commencement speakers quote great minds like Marie Curie: "Nothing in life is to be feared, it is only to be understood. Now is the time to understand more, so that we may fear less."

Albert Einstein: "Your imagination is your preview of life's coming attractions."

Or Yoda: "Do. Or do not. There is no try."

They share words from creative minds like composer Frederic Chopin: "Simplicity is the final achievement. After one has played a vast quantity of notes and more notes, it is simplicity that emerges as the crowning reward of art."

Or dancer Martha Graham: "There is a vitality, a life force, a quickening that is translated through you into action, and because there is only one of you in all time, this expression is unique. If you block it, it will never exist through any other medium and be lost. The world will not have it."

Holy people, like Mother Teresa, are often quoted to inspire the best in others: "In this life we cannot do great things. We can only do small things with great love." And Gandhi: "Live as if you were to die tomorrow. Learn as if you were to live forever."

Famous athletes are cited, like baseball great Babe Ruth, who said, "It's hard to beat a person who never gives up." Hockey player Wayne Gretzky: "You miss 100 percent of the shots you don't take." Or tennis star Arthur Ashe: "Start where you are. Use what you have. Do what you can."

Writers still inspire. Shakespeare: "This above all: To thine own self be true." J. K. Rowling, who created Harry Potter: "We do not need magic to change the world, we carry all the power we need inside ourselves already: we have the power to imagine better." And poet Maya Angelou: "Be courageous, adventurous. Give us a tomorrow, more than we deserve."

What would you tell someone launching a new life? I'd tell them this:

Life is like a snow globe.

Find your center and fortify it. You're not alone in there, even when you feel all alone in this big, wild, wonderful world. There is something or someone Higher than you. Call it God, Spirit, Energy, Shakti. It doesn't matter what you call it. It matters that you connect with it and stay connected.

That inner life is the most important part of your whole life. That part never moves, never falters, never fails, never falls. The world will shake your snow globe, and it is going to look and feel like everything is falling apart all around you and breaking into a million little pieces. Things will fall and scatter and leave you feeling disoriented, disappointed, and discombobulated.

Friendships you thought would last forever fade away. Lovers will leave or let you down. Your own family might even betray you for a time. Jobs will come and go. And don't even get me started on the stock market, global warming, and the politics of division.

But that center will always hold, so hold onto it.

If you can't get rid of your fears, bring them with you.

People will tell you to have no fear. That's wishful thinking. If you're living a bold life, you'll be afraid. So be afraid bigger and bolder, so bold that your fears become afraid of you.

I've been afraid my whole life, but I didn't let it stop me from living my best life. I've prayed every sort of prayer for God to remove my fears. A lot of them vanished. Then new ones popped up, like that Whac-A-Mole arcade game where as soon as you smack a mole with the mallet, another one pops up.

I decided I'm not waiting to be confident or sure. I just start pounding away with that mallet and say, "Come on fear, we've got a deadline. Let's go write this book." Or, "Get on the plane, fear, we're going to Poland."

Afraid of flying? Buckle up fear in the seat next to you. Squeeze that belt tight because you're going anyway. Afraid of falling in love? Buy fear a drink at the bar and let fear look for someone else to bother tonight. Don't let it keep you under the covers all day long. Yes, life is scary. So what? People pay to be scared. That's why they make roller coasters and horror movies.

Life is messy. Find the magic tucked in the mess.

I was a total mess. Some days I still am, and I'm okay with that.

In high school, I was good at one thing: drinking. I drank to ease the pain of life until the drinking caused more pain. And yet, when I look back now, I see the magic still got in. There were many magicians, only they called them teachers. They reached out, they blessed my life in ways big and small. Mr. Maske, my choir teacher, gave me a love of music. Mr. Ricco, my English teacher, taught me to love writing. Mr. Roberto, my biology teacher, taught me to love and respect all life, no matter how small.

In college, I gave myself a do-over. I tried to create a new life, but I went from Dean's list to academic probation. When chemistry got too hard, I quit going to class and played euchre in the student center. I flunked chemistry, got D's in zoology and child psychology. Then I got pregnant at 21 and dropped out of school.

A new life began. I got sober at 25. I went back to college, and Kent State University gave me a clean start, erased my bad grades with their "academic forgiveness" policy. I changed my major six times before choosing journalism, which led to writing columns and books full of graduation advice for messy people like me.

Along the way, I got a master's degree in religious studies and fell in love with the God of my joy, a God who loves me no matter how messy I am.

That baby I had at 21 is now 46. She gave me three grandchildren who make beautiful messes all over their house and mine.

We're each a messy masterpiece. We're supposed to embrace our unique, original mess and give thanks for all of it and share it with the world to make our difference. Not just any difference, but ours.

So, congratulations on whatever you are launching next.

Go wild and make a beautiful mess of your life.

39

If you have to grow older, you might as well grow bolder.

The Beatles ruined it.

No one can turn 64 without feeling old.

When you close in on that number, that song keeps running through your mind. Not quite running, more like jogging slowly or walking briskly or strolling.

The lyrics used to amuse me, especially when other people hit that mile marker, like my husband and older siblings. The year I turned 64, the words make me cringe. "Will you still need me, will you still feed me, when I'm sixty-four?"

It is comforting that the man who wrote the song is still rocking into his 80s.

I do celebrate growing old. A year after I finished chemo and radiation for breast cancer at age 41, I felt terrible stabbing pains in my lower back. The oncologist ordered a bone scan. I prepared myself for the worst: bone cancer.

The technician announced, "You have arthritis in a disc in your back."

I jumped with glee. Woo hoo! I have arthritis!

I got busy doing back exercises, strengthened the muscles

around my spine, and could still give my granddaughters pig-gyback rides, even when they were 9 and 11. While I can no longer beat my teenage grandson at basketball, I still try and get in the game.

During the pandemic, I hit the brakes on coloring my hair and let it go naturally gray. When our governor ordered the closing of barber shops and hair salons, a friend wrote on Facebook, "It's about to get ugly out there!"

Nah. I look in the mirror and see the silver lining. I "get to" grow old. Today is the best I'm ever going to look. Today, I'm the youngest I will ever be. You, too.

Birthdays are a time to freshen up. To wear bolder colors. To stand a little taller. To walk a little farther. I tell everyone, I "get" to grow old. Gray hair is no biggie when you've been bald at 41 from chemo.

Of course, there are things I'd like to improve to keep my body healthy for the long haul. We've all heard the quote, "If I had known I was going to live this long, I would have taken better care of myself."

Like most people, I treat my car better than my own body. My car never runs out of gas, but I do. I skimp on sleep and forget to eat or don't always put the right fuel in my body. I want to make better choices to eat clean, move more, and sleep when I'm tired.

I want to make more time for friends, especially after losing so many great ones this past decade. The older you get, the more likely you are to lose someone you love. It's guaranteed unless you die first. You don't know who you will lose, so all you can do is love them all better.

One day you will lose your parents, siblings, or spouse. Make peace with them now. One day your children or grandchildren will be moving away from you into their own lives. Give them the best of you now because all you have is now.

Turning older is both a grand exit and a beautiful beginning. I love this quote from my favorite Irish writer, John O'Donohue:

"At any time you can ask yourself: At which threshold am I now standing? At this time in my life, what am I leaving? Where am I about to enter? What is preventing me from crossing my next threshold? What gift would enable me to do it? A threshold is not a simple boundary; it is a frontier that divides two different territories, rhythms and atmospheres."

A frontier. That's what old age is. A new frontier.

When I turned 50, I wrote the top 50 lessons life taught me. Here are some lessons I've learned since then:

Keep your heart wide open. Nothing and no one are ever worth closing it over. Nothing. Life is too short to close it. Relax and stay open. No matter what.

Let go or be dragged. Pretty much everything I let go of has claw marks on it. God pries my fingers off it one by one. Old age allows me to laugh at all the challenges that made me into who I am, but first shattered who I was.

Every experience is worth having. Every mess, mistake, or misfortune becomes a great gift when you share it to help another. It's your own personal lottery ticket: You cash it in to give away and make everyone a winner.

Declutter now so your kids won't have to. Release all that stuff now. Don't make them spend weeks of their life clearing out your basement and garage after you're gone.

God is always with you. In the emergency room. In the

waiting room. In the recovery room. In the hospice bed. If you're feeling lost, remember: God isn't the one who moved.

The secret to true peace is to have no preferences. A great Zen master said, "The Great Way is not difficult for those who have no preferences." Practice having no preferences. Let life choose and surprise you.

Before saying yes, ask yourself what you're giving up to say yes. Is it worth the exchange? This is your life you're trading.

"No" is a complete and final sentence. Writer Anne Lamott was right. You don't need to give excuses. Saying "no" is enough.

All the love you will ever need is already inside of you. It's not in the person you married or want to find. The Source of all love flows within. The only one blocking it is you. It's like you're standing on a garden hose or twisting it off with fears and resentments. Relax and that love will flow like a fountain.

Allow. Allow life to simply unfold. Allow others to be right. Allow others to be wrong. Allow yourself to cry. Allow life to be weird and wonky. Allow every precious experience to pass all the way through you and be done with it.

Sleep is a gift you give yourself. My personality degrades when I don't get enough sleep. If you feel stressed out, take a nap and pray for a spiritual awakening.

The moment you are in is the most important moment. You're missing the present moment every time you're on your cell phone taking a picture of it or escaping it because you're bored. Savor here, savor now.

You want a big life mission? This is it.

The moments matter the most.

Don't waste them.

40

When you surrender to the Universe, you always win.

Surrender.

That has become one of my favorite words. I use it as a mantra, all day long.

It's a powerful word.

Actually, author Michael Singer chose it for me. He's a nice Jewish boy who now lives like a Buddhist. Transformed by a life of meditation and yoga, he teaches people how to let go of all their preferences and let life choose what is best for them.

He wrote two books that I read often, *The Surrender Experiment* and *The Untethered Soul*. One year I made a deep commitment to surrender. To keep my heart open. Once I did, I became painfully aware of how often it shuts.

It closes on the driver who won't let me pass. On the mosquito dining on my elbow. On the stranger playing music too loudly.

I listened to an eight-part series of Singer's talks on Sounds True and at the end said, "I'm in."

Then my world turned upside down.

It was all good.

I even had to surrender the good. He believes that if we stop clinging to what we think we want and stop resisting what we don't want, we will be free to accept whatever the Universe gives us. Give it a try. You'll be amazed at what happens next.

I often cling to the good. I replay it and take videos and pictures of it instead of soaking up the experience right as it is happening. I used to save my happiest moment of the day in a big clear crystal vase to read at the end of the year. One day the vase was empty. The cleaning lady tossed it all out.

At first my heart sank. Oh no, all my happiness gone! Then I laughed. The Universe made me let go, even of the good stuff. Faith means trusting there is always more good.

It's like manna from heaven. The Bible tells the story this way: When the people of Israel were being led through the wilderness to the Promised Land, they were hungry, and bread fell from heaven. Voilà! God provided. When they tried to save it for the next day, it went bad. Who wants to eat moldy bread?

The lesson? Trust the Source to provide for your daily needs. The Lord's Prayer says, "Give us this day our daily bread." Not enough loaves to last all month.

Surrender to that Source. Walk out on that faith and believe it will hold you.

Here's what happened when I did.

My sister, Theresa, and her husband decided to move to Cleveland from their home in Indiana. I spent a few days on the online real estate site Zillow one March looking for the right home. I sent her various links, but nothing felt quite right. One day, when I was driving by one of the lakes in Cleveland Heights, I saw a lovely home with a For Sale sign in the yard. I sent her the Zillow link.

She said it wasn't right for them but wrote, "This house is like the gold standard of houses!"

Really? What did she mean by that? I clicked on the link I had sent her and scanned all the photos: The house was listed as a mid-century modern Cape Cod across from a lake. It had central air conditioning, first-floor laundry with a washer and dryer, and a first-floor primary bedroom and bath, something we would need as we grow old. Our current home had three floors and no bedroom on the first floor, no air conditioning, and no full bathroom on the first floor.

This new house was perfect for us. But we weren't looking. But maybe it was time. So I took it to prayer, surrendered the outcome, and called the agent listed on Zillow. He was blunt.

"It's sold. It says pending sale, but it's sold. I don't even know why it's listed," the man said. He didn't even bother to get my name and phone number, so I believed him.

So I went back to prayer and said, "Thanks, God, for showing me this house. Keep us in mind if it ever goes for sale again." Then I let it go. No wishing. No whining. I totally surrendered it.

When I told my daughter about the house, she said her Realtor sold that house to its current owners and suggested the agent might let me see it. At first I closed my heart. Why bother getting my hopes up just to be disappointed? It's already sold. Then I opened my heart and my mind. Why not take a look just for the fun of it?

The Realtor took me through it. Wow. Giant windows revealed a huge backyard and front view of the lake, plus there were skylights in the family room. Sunlight poured in during the day. At night you could see the stars. It had a remote-control gas fireplace. It was in the same price range as the house we owned but with no basement or third floor.

So I surrendered again. I prayed and thanked God for showing me the inside of the house. Maybe five years from now these new owners might move and this house would be available when we were ready to move.

The next day the Realtor texted me. The buyers backed out. The house needed a buyer. It was going back on the market in two days. Did I want it?

What?! We had 48 hours to decide. We had 48 hours to bid on the house before it went back on the market. Meanwhile, there was no "we." I had looked at it alone. My husband had no idea I had even looked at the house, a house I had surrendered twice already.

So I went back to prayer to surrender it a third time. He might not want to leave the house we had lived in for 23 years. We had celebrated so many holidays there and loved it. So I surrendered and trusted whatever happened next. If I told him and he hated the idea, I would accept it.

He loved it.

We didn't love that it didn't have a basement, but even that turned into a gift. We downsized what we owned, donating three truckloads to a local charity, surrendering who we used to be. Our house sold in a month. We moved that June of 2019. Same city, just a mile closer to the grandkids. My sister and her husband found their perfect home five minutes away.

When we tell our friends we moved, they all say, "We didn't know you were looking."

Neither did we.

Fortunately, the Universe was.

41

Receiving is a gift, too.

There are two kinds of people: those who love to give gifts, and those who love to receive them.

I'm good at giving gifts but terrible at receiving them.

As soon as someone gives me a gift, I get nervous. *Is it really for me?* I usually ask, then check the tag or name on the card to be sure. *Can I really trust it? Is it a mistake? Could it be a trick?*

As soon as I open it, I wonder who might need or want it more than I do. I used to feel so unworthy receiving gifts. They made me uncomfortable. I've learned to practice receiving. Now I stop, pause, open my heart, and make sure it is in receiving mode to let the joy in.

Gifts make some people feel vulnerable. A dear friend had a father who was abusive. When he graduated high school, his dad gave him a wrapped gift. What a pleasant surprise, until he opened it and saw what was inside: toilet paper. His dad said it was for all the times his son crapped on him.

I never had anything so cruel happen, but my dad was fond of crushing our toys if we fought over them. I loved my toy dollhouse. One day my sister and I were arguing over it, so my dad stomped the doll house into a crumpled sheet of metal and tossed it aside.

Those kinds of moments warn you not to get too attached to anything you are given. Then no one has the power to hurt you.

Compliments are also tough to receive. If someone complimented a blouse, I used to diminish the compliment by telling them I bought it on sale or that it was old. Over the years, I've learned to really hear their words, pause a few seconds, let them land on my heart, then simply say, "Thank you."

I've since made a conscious effort to receive every note or card, to consider the time someone spent going to the store, choosing it, writing on it, and mailing it.

When I get flowers now, I inhale each one, touch the petals, and change the water daily to enjoy them.

My grandkids love to give me gifts. Asher once saved his money to buy me an ice cream cone. He carried a little bag with his money jingling at the bottom. I so wanted to pay for the cone and let him keep the money, but that would have robbed him of the gift of giving. It was the best cone ever.

When you receive a gift, you receive a bit of someone's love.

What a gift it is. But receiving also means someone else is in control of the giving, and you have to go with the flow. When you do, life can surprise you with the greatest gift of all.

It happened to me one February, three months before my 60th birthday. I had signed in to visit my mom at her assisted living home when I saw in the registry the names Matt and Patricia Brett.

My brother had been here from Chicago? My sister was in town from New York City? I called them. No answer. Hmm.

They might still be in the parking lot. But they didn't return my calls.

When I visited my mom, she said, "Oh, this has been such a great day! Patricia was here from New York and Matt was here from Chicago. You just missed them."

I texted them. Still no answer.

I started to feel hurt. Why didn't they tell me they were in town? Instead of turning into Cry Baby Boo Boo, I tried to focus on my visit with mom.

On the drive home I called my daughter. Maybe Gabrielle could solve this puzzle. She listened, then invited me to drop by her house.

Finally, Matt texted me: *"Cleveland? Sounds fishy...impostors!"* And a text from Patricia popped up: *"Someone stole my identity!"*

I was talking to Gabrielle when Matt and Patricia suddenly leaped into the room. What?! Gabe had a strange twinkle in her eyes. Phase I is complete, she said. There was more?

"Just go with the flow. Be like a river," Gabe said. Okay. I'd give it a try. We went out to eat, but no one would say why they were in town.

On Monday, I picked up my granddaughters from preschool and brought them to Gabrielle's. Her front door opened to a strange totem pole of heads: Mike and Chris. My brother and his wife drove up from Columbus. Were they all gathering to have an intervention on me?

"Just go with the flow. Be a river," Gabrielle said. It was starting to feel like a weird trust exercise, but I went along with it. Instead of trying to figure out what was going on, I decided to just receive it and savor it.

I put my work aside and made my family a priority since

they were making me one. We ate, laughed, talked, and played games. That evening, my son-in-law left on a secret mission. When he came back, my sister Joan walked in the room.

From Phoenix.

They all grinned. I nearly fell off the chair. Still, no one revealed a thing.

On Tuesday, we went to the Cleveland Museum of Art. I expected the rest of my siblings to leap out from behind a Rodin. Nope. But when we pulled up to Gabrielle's house for lunch, some nut was standing in the middle of the road, directing traffic with two Star Wars lightsabers. It was my sister Theresa. From Evansville, Indiana, a seven-hour drive.

Before I could get out of the car, my sister Mary Jo, from Columbus, walked up with a dish towel draped over her arm.

"May I take your lunch order?" she asked.

No one would tell me what was going on. Not even Asher, my grandson and greatest ally. I tried to bribe him with a dollar.

"No," he said.

"Will you tell me for ten?" He grinned, then his better angels took over. He declined.

Gabrielle smiled. It was starting to look a bit evil, that smile.

"Just be like a river. Go with the flow," she said for the 80th time. So I did.

At 5 p.m., we went out for dinner. There were 12 adults around the table. They all knew what was going on except me.

Gabrielle announced we were gathered to celebrate my 60th birthday, which was in late May. She thanked everyone for taking the time and expense to be here. Then she handed me a gift box.

Wow, I felt so loved. They came all this way to surprise me

and took off work for days. But why not on a weekend? It was Tuesday.

Inside the box was a puzzle made from a black and white photo. I pieced it together. It was an old photo that sort of resembled a young Bruce Springsteen or Scott Baio from that *Joanie Loves Chachi* TV show. Gabe handed me two missing pieces.

The River.

Bruce Springsteen.

I screamed. It was the cover of The River album. The Boss was in Cleveland for The River Tour. Tonight? YES. Tonight. And we were *all* going. I finally got it: Flow like *The River.*

The flow carried us to the Q, the multipurpose arena in downtown Cleveland. We sang. We danced. We clapped. We swayed. We cheered. I have never felt so loved by them all. I couldn't stop looking at their smiles.

Springsteen played for three hours without a break. The last hour felt like the longest encore in history. The next day I was still pinching myself.

Not over his music, but over the greatest gift my family gave me, one I have finally learned to receive with my whole heart: their presence.

And the best gift I can give them is to receive it.

42

Listen to the tug on your heart.

My mom just wanted to go Home.

Actually, she had wanted to die at her home at 420 Sycamore Street, at the house we always called 420, but she was now in an Alzheimer's care unit, so her wish to "die at 420" was impossible.

I tried to help her spiritually and pray my mom home.

Every night, I would get quiet and try to meet her soul in prayer and tell her it was okay to go home. If you can spiritually help someone die, that's what I tried to do.

I kept giving her permission to go, kept asking if there was anything unfinished. She was ready. We were ready. I offered her my spiritual heart and hand to carry her home. My spirit told her spirit, *Mom, you are loved. It's okay to go.*

That November, my sibs and I had planned to gather in Virginia to celebrate my younger brother's 50th birthday. We had all cleared the weekend to gather, but something in me wondered if we were supposed to gather elsewhere.

My husband kept saying my mom could go to 100. Alzheimer's had damaged her brain, but the rest of her body was fine. She had never broken a hip, never had a body part replaced, and was never in the hospital for anything in her old age.

Then one Sunday a nurse from Light of Hearts care center called. My mom had a fever and trouble with her balance. They thought she might have a urinary tract infection and planned for her to see the doctor the next day. Something tugged at my heart and told me to go visit.

When I visited her that Sunday evening, her hands were shaking. Those hands never shook. Those delicate hands that raised 11 children looked fragile, but they were mighty. Not this day. They trembled like butterfly wings over her heart.

While my husband talked to her, I found the staff and told them my concerns and asked them to look in on her more often through the night.

When I went back to her room, I sat next to her on the couch and gave her my full presence. I listened with love to all those stories I had heard 100 times. I touched that white wispy hair and held her frail hands, those hands that changed endless diapers and cooked countless meals and rolled out endless nut rolls for Christmas and crocheted dozens of slippers, scarves, and hats for the poor.

That tug on my heart said, *If this is your last visit, make it count.* So I kept my hand on her back, stroked it gently, and tried to pour all the love I had in me into her. The truth is, I was trying to hold on to the mother I had so often wanted to let go of, this mother I could finally, finally, love.

As we sat on the couch, I asked my husband to take a picture of us. My husband rarely came to visit her with me. In fact, he never came just to visit; it was usually to pick her up or drop her off. Most pictures I took of the two of us were selfies because it was just the two of us. He snapped away. I'm so grateful he did.

Even though Mom was trembling and wobbly, she was faithful as always and unafraid and ready to go home.

"I'm waiting for God to send me an angel," she said.

"Maybe it will be Frankie," I told her.

She still talked about her beloved collie from childhood. For weeks I had prayed for Dad to escort her home. I even prayed to her brothers, her sister, and sisters-in-law. Nothing had worked. Maybe Frankie could lead her home.

"If you see Frankie, follow him home," I told her.

I thanked her for everything she did right as a mom, especially for giving me five brothers and five sisters. Then I hugged her like I would never see her again.

I wouldn't.

The phone rang at 4:30 a.m. I thought the sound was my husband's alarm clock ringing until he handed me the phone. He said, "Oh my God, you were right."

The woman on the phone was crying.

"I'm so sorry," she said. "Your mother passed." She sounded brokenhearted.

They discovered her when they were doing their routine checks. I thanked the woman and said that it was okay, that Mom was ready and that I was sorry for their loss, too. The staff saw her more often than any of us did and truly loved her.

I quickly dressed and drove to Light of Hearts in the dark as fast as I could. On the drive there, I phoned two brothers who had been her powers of attorney and broke the news. I needed to tell someone to make it real. Our Mom was gone.

A uniformed police officer met me at the door.

"You can't go in," he said. What?

"We have to see if it's a coroner's case," he said. I almost laughed. Did he really think someone had sneaked into the locked Alzheimer's Unit and killed my mother?

"Can I at least be near her room, just to be present?" I asked.

He let me through the locked door to her apartment where the EMS unit waited for a doctor to confirm the cause of death. The doctor ruled it was a massive heart attack.

While I waited, I made the waiting a prayer. Her spirit might still be here. When they let me in, her nightlight statue of Mary glowed on her dresser. I knelt next to her and put my hand on her back. Her body was still warm. What a blessing to feel her warmth one last time. It was her last gift to me. I thanked her for the blessing she was to me and to all of us.

I felt at peace with her passing, with who she was and who she wasn't. I thanked her for loving us, then said the prayers she would have wanted to hear, the Our Father, Hail Mary, and Glory Be.

I wouldn't leave until the funeral home arrived to transport her body. While I waited, I called each of my brothers and sisters. I had sent them all an email just hours earlier updating them on her condition after my visit with her:

> Light of Hearts called me today to say Mom had trouble with her balance today, that she had some abdominal pain and had a slight fever. They are keeping a close eye on her and checking her for a urinary tract infection.
>
> I visited her tonight with Bruce. She said she was doing fine, but her hands were very shaky and she kept patting her heart. She could barely lift herself off the couch. She seemed much weaker than last week when I saw her.
>
> I talked to one of the nurses tonight and shared my con-

cerns. He said the staff would check on her more often to see if she needs any help.

I know conversations are difficult, but if you can, pop a card in the mail or give her a quick call. She still jots down in her daybook when one of you calls. It helps her savor it and remember.

She said she's waiting for God to send an angel to get her. I told her it could be Frankie, her beloved collie, and told her to follow him home. I have a feeling that might happen in the coming weeks.

Before I left, I gave her many hugs, patted her back and thanked her for everything she did right as a mom, mostly for giving us each other.

I'll keep you posted if anything changes.

Everything just changed.

Everything.

I kept looking at the clock. Somehow, I expected time to stop, expected time to take its last breath, too, but the hands kept moving, even though inside of me time felt altered forever.

As the funeral home employees wheeled her out, I saw a twinkle in her barely open eyes. It was just the reflection from the hall light above, but I felt it was her thanking me for carrying her all the way home.

And although she felt God betrayed her by not letting her die in her sleep at her beloved home, 420, He didn't forget her.

When I went to the funeral home the next day, they showed me the death certificate for Mary Jane Brett. Time of death? 4:20.48.

43

*God's plan for other people
is none of your business.*

My mom had a secret life.

We found out the extent of it after she died.

At the funeral home, Sister Regina, Mom's spiritual best friend, had shared the day her spiritual group talked about Mother Mary. She had asked all the residents to bring something to do with Mary, a rosary or holy card or book.

My mom brought a small white statue of Mary. Then Mom mesmerized them all. She held the statue up and told the group, "I wonder what Mary is praying for. Is she praying for Jesus? Is she praying for the neighbors?" Even though Alzheimer's had put the brakes on her brain, her soul was still searching for more God.

The Sunday after the funeral, we held a thank-you reception for the staff at Light of Hearts. My sister ordered a cake that read, "Thanks for loving our mother." We filled two tables with food, drinks, and desserts. The staff streamed in to eat and to tell us stories about Mom. We thought we were giving them a gift. It turns out they gave us one.

Their tears. That was their gift.

They cried over losing our mother. They told endless stories about what a loving mother she had been to them. She was like a second mother to them.

Really? We looked at each other in shock. Our mom? Motherly?

We were stunned. It turns out she was needed there by them.

There she got to be a new person. Someone else. Someone new. Miss Mary. We heard story upon story about how Miss Mary blessed their lives, how she listened to their woes, taught them to crochet, gave them wisdom to settle family feuds. She would stay up late and chat with them, and if they heard someone coming, she'd run back to her room like a child. The resident who wailed and moaned and pounded on the locked door? Mom would lead her back to her room. She was the ambassador of the Memory Unit.

God called her here to mother them. This woman who couldn't mother me mothered them all. It turned out my mom was supposed to be here. We didn't put her here. God did, not to protect her, but to use her. She wasn't finished with her life yet. She still had a mission, a calling, and it was none of our business. Most things aren't.

This place was like a monastery for this holy woman so full of holes. Here she prayed the rosary every day and lived like a monk, sleeping in a small twin bed surrounded by rosaries, statues, and her library of books on the psalms, parables, and bibles.

And we heard how grateful Mom was to the staff that fixed her meals, did her laundry, cleaned her apartment, and took her for scenic drives and ice cream runs.

All that guilt over "putting her there" as if it were a warehouse or waiting room to a heaven that took so long to call her number, all that guilt vanished. Mom belonged there. God had a plan for that chapter of her life, and we weren't in it. Here, she completed her life. She was a light here, a beacon in Room 141.

We bagged up all her sweaters, slacks, and boxed up her books. We donated everything she owned to the Light of Hearts resale shop and gave skeins of yarn to the aide Mom taught to crochet. The woman cried as if we had given her a bag full of money.

Then I went to the activity room to give Mom's best friend her most prized possession. It took me back in time . . .

It's funny the memories that come to you when you're seeing your father's face for the very last time. I remembered how, when his own father lay dying in the county home, a place that smelled of urine and ammonia, my dad would talk to him like they were having a conversation, even though a stroke had stolen my grandpa's Irish brogue.

One day my dad wandered across the hall to talk to a man who had no visitors. Catholics normally don't go around witnessing and asking people whether they've accepted Jesus as their savior, but Dad gathered up the lost sheep in his own way. When he learned that the man was a fallen Catholic, my dad wanted to make sure he would land in the right place when he died, so he gave him a rosary. My dad knew that when the man died, the rosary would tip them off to call a priest and give him the Last Rites sacrament, to pray him home.

For my family, the rosary wasn't just a connection to God; it was a lifeline. My great grandma prayed it in her cottage near Castlebar, Ireland, prayed by the fireplace, probably for food.

My grandparents prayed it when my dad was flying over Burma as a tail gunner, for his safe return. My dad prayed it with his 11 children, for peace and quiet.

When one sister got married, my dad was too sick to fly to New York to walk her down the aisle, so she carried his rosary. When he died a few months later, we prayed the Hail Mary at the funeral home for the man who tucked a rosary under our pillows. On nights I can't sleep, I'll pray one for whoever needs a prayer most.

My first rosary beads glittered like diamonds. That's what I thought they were, back when I was seven and got one for my First Communion. Back then I hated saying the rosary. We had to kneel along the couch in our nighties and jammies, our heads bowed like pious monks until a brother elbowed you or a sister giggled between Hail Marys, which my dad did not appreciate and let us know later with his belt.

We never reflected on the mysteries of Jesus' life. The only mystery we pondered was why Mary couldn't hear us the first time we said the prayer. Why did we have to say it 50 times? We used to race to see who could say them the fastest until we saw that movie where Mary shows up to the poor kids of Fatima, and they stop mumbling the rosary and become saints.

I was tempted to keep my mom's rosary, the one she carried with her every single day, but someone else needed it more.

Jean.

Jean was Mom's best friend at Light of Hearts.

Because of Alzheimer's, Mom kept reintroducing me to Jean at every visit. The short woman with the blank face would barely look up, her brain a vacant canvas, but my mom always talked to her. Jean had several strokes that stole her speech.

Mom always told me the same story:

"She can't talk. She doesn't say anything, so I talk to her every day." Then my mom would kiss Jean on the head. The woman never said a word, but my mom never stopped doing it. Maybe her mission there was to love Jean. Maybe it was that simple. To love one person.

Then one day the story had a different ending. One day, after my mom kissed Jean on the head, this woman who could no longer speak looked up at my mom and said, "I love you."

I always wondered if it were Alzheimer's fiction, that it was what Mom wanted to hear, but at that memorial reception, the staff confirmed it. They had witnessed it.

"I was there," an aide told me. It really had happened and had stunned them all.

So I walked to the activity room, to the big dining room where our Mother Mary statue stood sentry in the corner, that statue that lived in our house for so long. We had donated it to bless the place and help her feel more at home. I went there to say goodbye to Jean.

Part of me wanted to keep Mom's rosary since it was the one thing she carried every day and was her umbilical cord to God. But Jean needed it more than I did. I also took one of the last blankets that Mom had crocheted.

A worker was spoon-feeding Jean, who sat slumped over in her chair. I knelt next to her. I told her how much she meant to my mom. I wanted to make sure she understood that my mom had died, and that's why she wouldn't be seeing her anymore. I didn't want Jean to think my mom was ignoring her presence here.

"My mom would want you to have this. My mom loved you.

She died, so you won't see her anymore," I said as I gave her the rosary and set the afghan on her lap, then gave her a kiss on the forehead, just like Mom did.

Not long after, I got the call. Jean had died in her sleep.

I drove to Light of Hearts for the funeral. The hearse in front of the building reminded me of the one that picked up Mom. I signed in, walked to chapel, and sat under that brilliant blue dove.

Jean in the casket looked lovelier than she had in life. She had just completed her mission here.

Sr. Regina told a Jean story I had never heard. She mentioned how Jean had several strokes, and each one took more of her ability to speak. One day they were gathered to discuss the Bible. The reading was about Jesus and a man blind from birth.

His disciples asked, "Rabbi, who sinned, this man or his parents, that he was born blind?"

Jesus answered, "Neither this man nor his parents sinned, but this happened so that the works of God might be displayed in him."

When the nun asked if anyone wanted to share what the reading meant to them, Jean stood up, all four-foot-two of her. She held her hands out in front of her, opened them wide, and said one word: "This."

This.

Like that blind man, she was a gift, as is. She was a vessel for God's grace.

This.

This is all the glory of God. Even the messy parts. Even the terrible. The best life has to offer is sometimes tucked in the terrible that it allows.

I cried in the chapel. Sad that my mom's best friend was gone. Sad for all the sad people of the world. Sad for all the "this" I had missed all along.

And I cried tears of gratitude for every one of those mighty, messy works of God standing right smack in front of me.

44

Your presence is
what matters most.

It was the worst Christmas ever until my mother died and redeemed it.

The holiday had started off so perfectly. My sister drove nine hours from Indiana to spend the holiday with us. On Christmas Eve, we drove to Little Italy where everyone in Cleveland and his brother were buying pignoli and pizzelle at Presti's Bakery.

It was a party scene, with people high-fiving and hugging. We were there to pick up cannoli for a family friend who was in hospice. We knew Dodie liked cannoli, so it was worth the wait. She was my brother's mother-in-law, but she had been to so many family events that it felt like she belonged to us all. The cashier called out Number 6; we were Number 35, but patience is what advent is about, waiting in joyful hope, so we didn't mind.

Then we drove to the hospice in Ravenna an hour away, singing carols in the car. I slowed down on the highway when the cars in front of me started hitting their brakes. Those red brake lights sent off a warning, and I heard a little voice inside, or maybe a little Christmas angel, say, "Look up."

In the rearview mirror, I saw black. The car behind was barreling toward us. I hit the gas and tried to swerve out of the way.

BAM!

The car slammed into us at 45 mph. The driver never braked. Our cars skidded across the highway. It was a Christmas miracle that no one was coming in the other lane and that no one was hurt—just our cars.

The airbag had deployed in his car, and the front end was smashed in all the way to the seats, but he was fine. The young man in his 20s didn't apologize, didn't ask if we were okay, didn't care that he had smashed my car. He seemed angry at me, as if it were my fault he had been too distracted to brake in time.

While I was busy praying for the serenity not to slap him silly, a lovely stranger pulled over to see if we were safe. My sister chatted with her and, not knowing if we would be able to get to the hospice, gave the woman the cannoli and asked her to drop it off at the hospice in case we didn't get there.

I called the police, and a state patrol officer arrived. He ticketed the other driver and called for two tow trucks. I called my insurance company. They couldn't get me a ride or a rental car. It was Christmas Eve. There were no taxis or Ubers available in Ravenna on Christmas Eve.

How would we get home?

My husband wasn't allowed to drive; he had just had major surgery for Crohn's disease. My daughter was hosting Christmas Eve dinner with her in-laws. I called my brother, who lived nearby. Once the cars were towed, he drove us to visit his mother-in-law, Dodie.

And what about the cannoli? We arrived, but it seemed the cannoli hadn't.

Dodie was pure joy. We laughed about the wreck, the missing cannoli, and talked about old times for an hour when it hit me: That kind stranger wouldn't have kept our cannoli. It must be here somewhere. So I went down to the front desk and asked the receptionist, "I know this is a strange question, but did anyone drop off any cannoli today?"

"Yes," she said. "It's upstairs." We checked a few nursing stations and finally found it. Dodie got her last Christmas cannoli.

After much laughter, my brother drove us to his house a few minutes away while I figured out how to get back home to Cleveland an hour away. My brother offered to drive me home when my daughter called crying. It was 9 p.m. and her youngest child, who was two, wouldn't sleep and was screaming like a banshee. When I told my daughter about my crash, she hopped in the car and brought her daughter along for the ride to pick us up.

On the drive home, I held my granddaughter's tiny hand as we looked at all the Christmas lights. She had never been outside this late to even see stars. It was truly magical.

On Christmas Day, we usually go to the grandkids' home to celebrate, but my husband was still recovering. The grandkids were planning to come over early, but they all needed naps, so they didn't arrive until dinnertime, so it just didn't feel like Christmas.

And then there was my mom.

The year before, I had wanted to give her a perfect Christmas. I had taken a tiny Charlie Brown tree to her apartment with little ornaments. She didn't seem interested in the holiday at all. I had wanted Christmas magic with her, to bring her to my house, to watch movies with the fireplace going and the tree lit up. It was my fantasy, not hers. I wept the whole way home from that visit.

This year, when everything was unraveling, I had my mom all day. It didn't feel magical. I didn't want to be with her all day. Mom had slipped into a negative loop, and it was tough to spend more than an hour with those angry stories on endless repeat. She came over at 1:00 and didn't leave till 7:30 p.m. A sibling who had offered to help with her changed plans and didn't show up. If you love a parent with Alzheimer's, you know that sometimes it's a joy to be around them and sometimes, well, it sucks.

Halfway through Christmas I sat down on the steps in the back hall and cried. This wasn't how Christmas was supposed to be: my husband upstairs asleep on pain meds, the grandkids at their house, my car in the shop for a month, and my mom here all day long.

Oh, it got worse. My sister ended up in the emergency room. She was still dizzy from the car crash. Maybe with a concussion. It would take her a few weeks to feel normal again.

So I did the best I could. I did what my mom did with us when we were kids. I put on Christmas carols. I served her cookies. We watched *White Christmas*, *It's a Wonderful Life*, and *Miracle on 34th Street*, all her favorites. She soaked up the twinkle lights on the tree, the decorations, the fireplace, and told me this was the best Christmas ever.

We didn't know it would be her last Christmas ever.

One none of us will ever forget.

Christmas can be messy. Ours didn't get redeemed that year.

It got redeemed the next year when she wasn't around to celebrate it. That first year without her, I was out Christmas shopping when a lovely necklace caught my eye and demolished me with the one simple word engraved on it: MOM.

And suddenly, it hit me all over again that she was gone. And I will never ever buy anyone a gift that says MOM because I don't have a mom anymore.

But mothers are the gift that never stops giving. My mom gave me one of the best gifts, one I will open every single Christmas. My mom gave me her love of Christmas.

She always played carols all through December, mostly Perry Como, Andy Williams, and Mitch Miller. She is the reason I know the words to every Christmas carol. She watched every Christmas special, from Charlie Brown to Rudolph, which is why I don't miss a single one of them and can quote nearly every line. She baked endless cookies, which is why I binge-bake batch after batch. She picked out special gifts for all 11 of us every year with no car, just a Sears catalog and Dad's checkbook. The last gift she ever gave me was her presence on that worst Christmas Day. She gave me her complete presence, all day long, and I gave her mine.

Presence. That is the greatest gift of all.

I didn't realize what a great gift that was until she was gone.

So from now on, and forevermore, whatever happens on Christmas, or whatever doesn't happen, I trust it will be the perfect gift.

It just might take a long time to receive it.

45

It's all a gift.

Y ou don't look 60.

That's what people kept saying the week I turned 60.

What is 60 supposed to look like?

Were they nearsighted or just too kind to notice the wrinkles and growing constellations of age spots? I swear they're freckles gone wild.

When my odometer rolled over to 60, I was thrilled to see it happen. After having cancer at 41, turning 60 was a "get to." I "get to" grow old. Plus it was kind of like watching the old car odometer roll over with that row of clicking white numbers all turning at once.

Turning 60 is a blast. You just have to decide that it is.

How can anyone resent growing old? To grow old is to live. I see 60 as a reboot. I get to relaunch the rest of my life.

So I made a bucket list, not for the rest of my life, but just for one year: Go on a retreat. Start doing yoga. Research my ancestry. Finish another book.

I put on it a trip to Ireland. Then I made a bucket list of 60 things to experience there: See the stars over Kerry. Ride a horse on the beach at Dingle. Kiss the rain in Killarney. Wander the streets of Claremorris where my grandma was born. Sit under a tree in Coole Park where Yeats wrote poetry. Buy an Irish flag. Leave sweets for the fairies. Read a poem every morning. Eat homemade brown bread and Irish butter for breakfast.

When I told my friend Derdriu about my trip, she was thrilled. She was born in Cahersiveen, County Kerry. She made me a soundtrack to Ireland with 60 of her favorite Irish songs on three CDs. My friend Sheryl went with me on the trip to make it a fun Girl Whirl.

Sixty was when I decided to take the reins of my life, to really own it, to be an active player, not a passive observer.

In Ireland, I did a weekend of yoga at a retreat center that had two beautiful Buddhas and a glass wall overlooking the sea. I rode a boat to Inishmore and brought home rocks for my fairy garden. I climbed 618 steps to the top of Skellig Michael to stand inside a beehive hut and pray Psalm 23, just like the monks did centuries ago.

At a fort near the Cliffs of Moher, I stacked up stones in a cairn and left my fears. One rock for all the fears my dad taught me (never ride a snowmobile, stay out of compact cars, everything fun can and will hurt you), one for Mom's (never run with scissors, always wear clean underwear for the ER doctors, and trim your bangs so you don't get pink eye). I left stones to forgive those who hurt me so I could open my heart wider to more love.

I no longer need a fort around my heart to protect me. The secret is not to build a wider moat or be a fiercer dragon or build thicker walls or skin. The secret is to believe at the deepest core of your being that your soul is unhurtable.

Everything that happens just makes it stronger. And that's why I'm here. To grow my soul.

Then I came home and officially turned 60. Instead of lying about my age, I threw myself a party. The idea came to me at a family funeral six months earlier. My nephew, who had lost his grandma Dodie, commented to me that funerals were depressing. I told him mine would be a blast. I would throw the mourners a party. I wanted a cotton candy machine, live Irish music, and the Rocket Car.

"Why don't you do that while you're alive?" he asked with a grin.

Why not? So I made a list of 60 people who bring me joy and invited them to celebrate this amazing gift of life. Then I booked the cotton candy machine, the New Barleycorn (who play the best Irish music in town), and the Rocket Car. After a local amusement park closed, someone took one of the "rockets" from a swinging space rocket ride and turned it into a car. It's like a rocket on wheels. Zipping along in that silly car down the street makes me feel like the most joyful child in the world. I wanted everyone to enjoy it.

Then on the day of the party, it rained. And rained.

My heart sank until I heard that morning that Erica Weiss died. And I couldn't be sad about the rain.

Erica and I got breast cancer the same year, back in 1998. We became sisters in this sorority no one wants to join. We were both bald at the same time, but she looked much more glamorous and always did, even after the cancer came back.

It was tough to wrap my head and heart around the fact that she was gone. She was four years younger than me, and so vibrantly loved her life and family.

I loved Erica's beauty and her love of beauty. She created art and took such great care of the artists whose work she displayed at Juma, a boutique and art gallery she created in Shaker Heights, Ohio.

My dear friend Kandis, who lost her husband to cancer, showed up at my party wearing a lovely black dress she bought from Juma. Kandis wore the dress with joy to honor Erica. That's what you do with loss. You transform it.

When you start losing people you love, you start loving life even more. You hug people tighter and longer. You laugh louder and live bolder, because this is it, ladies and gentlemen. This. Is. Your. Life.

Savor it. All of it, the awful and the awesome, the mess and the magic, the mistakes and the mystery.

So when the Rocket Car canceled because of rain, it didn't matter. When the cotton candy disintegrated in the rain, it didn't matter. When the band had to squeeze in the living room to play, it didn't matter.

I held my youngest grandbaby to my heart, and we danced like no one was watching, her fresh dimpled hand in mine and her cheek pressed against mine, and all was right with the world.

Because nothing can rain on your parade when sheer gratitude is what the parade is all about.

Acknowledgments

So many people loved me into the person who wrote this book. It is impossible to thank them all by name. My apologies to anyone I left out. I hope you feel my heart wrapped around yours saying thank you.

I offer the deepest gratitude to . . .

Every family member, neighbor, friend, teacher, fellow student, and coworker who left an imprint on my heart and soul, an imprint that will remain on anyone who reads this book.

All those who made me a writer, especially Sam Ricco, my ninth-grade English teacher, and writing mentors Bill O'Connor, Rich Osborne, Dick Feagler, Stuart Warner, Connie Schultz, and Thrity Umrigar, along with my professors at Kent State University and John Carroll University, and my *Cleveland Jewish News* team headed by Kevin Adelstein and Bob Jacobs, who offer a weekly home for my words.

Everyone who trusted me to share their stories in this book. You will never know how many lives you have transformed: Hal Becker, Lynda Corea, Ian Friedman, Greg Justice, Jon Sedor, Paula McLain, Katie O'Toole Smith, Yvonne Pointer, Glenn Proctor, Karen Sandstrom, Rob Snow, Katie Spotz, Sharon Sullivan, Sophie Sureau, Danielle Wiggins, and those in blessed memory, Father Patrick, Ed Rafferty, Tom Raithel, Beth Ray, Jim Samuels, and Robert E. Wood.

My spiritual guide Lynn McCown.

Publisher David Gray at Gray & Company, Publishers, and his talented team who helped launch and promote this book, especially copy editor Linda Cuckovich and graphic designer Brian Willse, who created the illustration for the book cover.

Writer and friend Ted Gup, who led me to agent David Black, who led me to my agent Linda Loewenthal, who serves as a human compass in the publishing world.

My Polish friends and publishing team at Insignis Media, who cheered me on during four book tours there and never let me forget that writing is a precious privilege and ministry that deserves my highest and best self.

All my friends, fans, and followers on Facebook, Instagram, Twitter, TikTok, Pinterest, and YouTube for showing up and showing me so much love and support.

The endless constellation of readers whose emails, posts, and prayers encourage me to keep writing.

Booksellers everywhere, especially Suzanne DeGaetano and her team at Mac's Backs on Coventry.

A big shout-out to librarians in tiny towns like Ravenna, Ohio, where I grew up. You gave me a passport to the world in that endless supply of free books.

My huge family, Brett Nation, for loving me and always finding the fun in the dysfunction. I love you all and am grateful God chose you for siblings, in-laws, outlaws, nieces, and nephews.

Special thanks to my brother, Matthew Brett, for creating the logo for my Substack blog *Little Detours with Regina Brett*.

And artist Vicki Prussak, whose weekly calls, friendship, and professional guidance sustained and inspired me through the writing of this book.

All my front-row friends in the Panera Group, New Hope, the Crooked River Archers, the Wild Women Warriors, and my sacred circle, including Katie O'Toole Smith, Sharon Sullivan, Derdriu Ring, Sherrie Petersen, Sheryl Harris, and Eileen Saffran.

Our three children and their spouses, Gabrielle and James, Ben and Melanie, Joe and Sarah.

My sacred three, my perfect joy, my grandchildren Asher, Ainsly, and River.

Bruce Hennes, my partner for life, my spouse, and my guardrail.

Gabrielle, my daughter, my soulmate, and my biggest miracle, who reminds me every day how much I am loved.

And, as always, endless gratitude to the Source of it all, the God of my joy, for every single moment of life.

About the Author

Regina Brett is the author of the *New York Times* bestseller *God Never Blinks: 50 Lessons for Life's Little Detours,* which has been published in over 24 languages.

She is also the author of *Be the Miracle: 50 Lessons for Making the Impossible Possible* and *God is Always Hiring: 50 Lessons for Finding Fulfilling Work*, and six more books exclusively published in Poland.

Regina is a breast cancer survivor, mother, stepmom, wife, and grandmother.

She became a journalist in 1986 and has been a newspaper columnist since 1994. She was twice named finalist for the Pulitzer Prize in Commentary. She writes regularly for the *Cleveland Jewish News*.

Regina has a bachelor's degree in journalism and a master's degree in religious studies. She lives in Cleveland, Ohio, with her husband and their goldendoodle, McIntyre.

Sign up for Regina's weekly inspirational newsletter at:
www.reginabrett.com

Follow her on social media:
Facebook: **ReginaBrettFans**
Instagram and X: **@reginabrett**